Language an ....ng
in Home and School

Edited by

ALAN DAVIES

Heinemann Educational Books
London

Heinemann Educational Books Ltd
22 Bedford Square, London WC1B 3HH
LONDON   EDINBURGH   MELBOURNE   AUCKLAND
HONG KONG   SINGAPORE   KUALA LUMPUR   NEW DELHI
IBADAN   NAIROBI   JOHANNESBURG
EXETER (NH)   KINGSTON   PORT OF SPAIN

British Library Cataloguing in Publication Data

Language and Learning in home and
  school. – (Language and learning series)
  1. Children – Language – Congresses
  I. Davies, Alan   II. Series
  401′.9   LB 1139.L3

ISBN 0–435–10192–7

Printed and bound in Great Britain by
Biddles Ltd, Guildford and King's Lynn

Contents

Acknowledgements

I am grateful to the publisher Keith Nettle for his advice and reassurance over the preparation of this volume and its two predecessors. I acknowledge also the encouragement of Bryan Dockrell of the Scottish Council for Research in Education at whose initiative the Language and Learning Seminars were set up; and I want to thank the contributors and other participants at the Stirling and Cardiff Seminars for their patience in waiting for this volume to appear. My thanks to Margaret Love who has done most of the typing for this volume and to Sara Davies and Ben Davies who worked on the indexes for Volumes 1 and 2, and to Megan Davies and Hester Davies who collated the bibliography and provided the index for this volume.

Foreword

The papers in this book were prepared for two seminars organized by a committee chaired by Dr W. B. Dockrell and sponsored by the Educational Research Board of the Social Science Research Council. The Board has supported several of these seminars in areas of research where there is a particularly rapid development of ideas which are thought likely to influence the future pattern of educational thinking. The topic of language and learning was an obvious choice for such a seminar, and a series of such seminars has been sponsored over the last few years. The last seminar, to which some of these papers relate, was specifically concerned with 'Language in the Home'.

The seminars have a dual purpose; to promote the exchange of information and discussion of new methodologies among research workers in these areas of inquiry; and to provide a stimulus to new and promising directions of research.

Inevitably, the size of a seminar group must be limited. But the discussion among the relatively small group of participants is of interest and value to a wider public – not only other research workers and students but also teachers and administrators – who have much to gain from eavesdropping on the debate. For them, this record of these seminars provides an up-to-date review of important issues. If it succeeds also in sharpening thinking and helping understanding of current trends of research on language and learning, the seminars will have fully achieved their purpose.

JACK WRIGLEY
Professor of Education, Reading University; Chairman SSRC Educational Research Board

CYRIL SMITH
Secretary, Social Science Research Council

Introduction

ALAN DAVIES

This volume, the third in a series* on language and learning, contains papers from two seminars organized by the Scottish Council for Research in Education and the SSRC (Educational Research Board) in Stirling (1978) and in Cardiff (1979). The theme of the Stirling seminar was the impact of educational research in language teaching and learning on practice by teachers and others. The theme of the Cardiff seminar was the influence of the home on children's language development. Since research inevitably focuses on language processes in the two main arenas of the child's life, the home and the school, and since it is not possible to take account of language development in the home without considering also the school, it seemed sensible in this present volume to bring together papers from both seminars in order to highlight the relationship between home and school, a relationship that is important for research workers and teachers who are concerned with language learning and teaching.

The realization in the 1960s of the poignancy of the disadvantage afflicting many children from ethnic minorities and lower social classes led to various attempts at explanation and to a range of remedial endeavours. One of the explanations that attracted attention and research focused on language. Children were disadvantaged, it was argued, because they were linguistically deprived: such deprivation was itself described as being a result *either* of a social (or dialect) difference *or* of an individual deficit, though of course it was never easy to limit difference to social causes or deficit to individual ones. The debate was polemical and, in a sense, trivial since it was partly a matter of definition of 'difference' and 'deficit'. Trivial or not, such polemic distracted attention from the serious issue of whether or not language was a cause of deprivation.

* Earlier volumes were: *Problems of Language and Learning*, ed. A. Davies, Heinemann, 1975; and, *Language and Learning in Early Childhood*, ed. A. Davies, Heinemann, 1977.

Whatever the theoretical position, a number of remedial projects were set up, largely in the pre-school, the best known of which were the Head Start programmes in the United States, and the Educationally Deprived Areas scheme and the language enrichment programmes of Joan Tough in the United Kingdom.

So much for the analysis and optimism of the 1960s. In the 1970s there was less optimism but perhaps more analysis. The results and the conclusions were conflicting. If we consider education generally and not just language, the views (e.g. Jencks 1972) were heavily nature dominated. The effects of schooling were found to be minimal; what mattered was genetic endowment and the primary influence of the home. For educationists that was a pessimistic conclusion, but perhaps a useful one too since the 1960s had probably exaggerated the potential for change of the school. Again, the results of Head Start were not encouraging, showing no difference over control groups for Head Start children in primary schools. The dominant influences on the child's progress seemed to be the child's innate endowment and the home; the school had no significant effect. On the other hand a later study (Rutter *et al.* 1979) with older children has suggested quite a different situation – that the school *is* instrumental in affecting children's progress.

More recent studies (Raven 1980; Bruner 1980) have helpfully indicated that there is considerable interaction between home and school, that both are necessary and that both influence children's progress. It is this interaction that is at the heart of the present volume. In Chapter 1 Rosen and Burgess bring together a set of three working papers concerned with language and learning in the inner city secondary school. Two things are of particular interest to us here. The first is the growing realization of the fact of language diversity, not only inter-linguistic but also inter-dialectal, a realization that is now widespread that *all* schools are multilingual; the second is the demonstration of how teachers and researchers can come together in a common endeavour to act on the language of schoolchildren. Rosen and Burgess's chapter suggests how a development project learns as it goes along and becomes in the real sense action research.

In Chapter 2 Hazel Francis takes up this issue of research on language teaching and its effect on teachers in early education. What Francis concludes is that the outcome of the considerable amount of research into language teaching has certainly been to focus attention on language but hardly at all on the research findings. What we get then is a phenomenon well known in the reading field, viz., a halo effect or a language 'drive'. This is welcome of course since it indicates (or creates) enthusiasm; but it may represent an ill-informed or indeed a false idea of language learning and therefore of language teaching, and as such may be counterproductive.

Tosi's paper (Chapter 3) reminds us of the special case of multi-lingualism among an ethnic minority and of the real difficulties of maintaining group (as opposed to individual) bilingualism. His chapter also complements the arguments of Rosen and Burgess that children's home language may be not only different from the official school language but also different from an added or superimposed second language. The case of the Bedford Italian community illuminates the problem of educational ministries and authorities in their genuine attempts to support a home language in school by raising the issue of just what the home language is. This then must be a very general problem if it is indeed true, as argued above, that all communities are multilingual–multidialectal.

In his critical review of research on intervention, Chazan (Chapter 4) is quite clear that intervention has a significant effect on the child's language progress at home. He favours the role of the Educational Home Visitor whose job it is to take the school to the home. Indeed, it is precisely the deliberateness of the link between school and home that Chazan underlines and it may be that the value of the Educational Home Visitor scheme is precisely that it provides a method for bringing home and school together.

John Raven's concern (Chapter 5) is with one Educational Home Visitor (EHV) scheme (in the Lothian Region) and its evaluation. As he points out, the EHV idea began with the problem of disadvantage in (among other things) Bronfenbrenner's perception that intervention programmes were more likely to succeed if the home – and especially the mother – were directly engaged. 'The objective . . . was to encourage the mothers to play a more active role in promoting the educational development of their children' (p. 79). The Lothian project was 'one of the largest of its kind in the world'. Raven's eloquent study shows that intervention does matter, that it changes people but that we cannot always be sure how it changes them. 'The Home Visitors have had a significant impact on the [lower socio-economic status] parents' priorities, and they have led them to feel better motivated to tackle their problems. Nevertheless, they have not been able to lead them to feel any more able to tackle their problems' (p. 118).

And Raven has two very salutary things to say about language, first that the importance of language in the adult–child relationship may be very small, that language is not as salient as it sometimes appears to be to linguists; and second that in intervention programmes it is not just a question of influencing language, getting more talk going on between mother and child, it is also and importantly a question of *what sort of talk*. It is no use, Raven argues, repeating at home the teacher-type talk of the typical nursery/primary school with its working-class ethos, lacking the insistence on individual independence of the 'middle-class value system'. Indeed Raven's conclusion seems at first dispiritingly circular; from EHVs in the home we find that after all it may be necessary for mothers to reach out and become part of the outside world in the form of the pre-school. But perhaps it is not so dispiriting since the purpose of the EHV scheme was precisely to strengthen this link.

Assessment of language as of other skills is so much a part of what we expect to happen in school that Ruth Clark's cautionary admonitions come as a shock (Chapter 6). Her subject is assessment in the home where she finds no place for formal or summative judgements. At the same time, of course, parents do make assessments of their children's speech in the sense that they put interpretations on what is said. No doubt these assessments are sometimes flawed or even blatantly wrong but, Clark insists, the parents are the best judges of that speech since they come closest to being native speakers of their children's idiolects. Clark urges the differential nature of speech, reminiscent in a way of Raven's argument about purpose. Clark's data clearly show that the child's awareness of language is more sensitive and complex in informal situations with a trusted adult, notably of course with mother or other caretaker. What is risky about such prominence being given to this particular dyadic interaction is that for parents and children context is probably more salient than language.

Hence the tendency is for parents (like all native speakers) to give an interpretation to *every* utterance whether or not it conforms to a linguistic code. It may, however, be that it is precisely through such elaboration of context that language is acquired; Clark is, after all, insistent on the importance of non-verbal systems in communication between parent and child, again reminding us of Raven's downgrading of language in child development.

The importance of the caretaker–child relation in language growth both in terms of speech or in terms of complexity is stressed again in Wells's chapter (Chapter 7). What he reminds us of, in a discussion of results that came out of an analysis of data collected in Bristol over a period of several years, is that the interaction between parent and child works both ways and that the parents' language is influenced by their children's.

Wells has taken his study on from the pre pre-school stage right into the primary school. There again, as he shows, the home – in terms of parent attitudes – influences children's attainment of literacy. Children in his study who do best at reading at age 7 are those whose parents talk most to them and who are themselves most interested in reading.

The division between home and school for the child may be much less clear-cut than for us adult observers. The child entering school, still at his egocentric stage, is at the centre of his own world. He takes that with him into the different scenes of life but those scenes may be much less vivid to him than we think. It may be that for him language development in school or home is constantly informed by the other place. Certainly, as teachers and analysts, we cannot afford to neglect the interpenetration for children's language of school with home and home with school.

1

Language in the Inner City: An Investigation

HAROLD ROSEN AND TONY BURGESS

1 Introduction

1.1   In 1976 in the English Department at the University of London Institute of Education we decided to undertake a project (unfunded) which would have as its focus a constellation of concerns that arise in inner-city schools and are in some way or another connected with language. We had in mind such concerns as dialect, bilingualism, linguistic diversity, cultural diversity, literacy, etc.

The whole project was, of necessity, modest in respect of the scale and intensity of its operations but ambitious in its theoretical and practical exploratory style of working. In particular, we attempted from the beginning to work in close partnership with teachers in schools, colleagues and researchers in other institutions, and ILEA Centres. Thus a minimally formal network was established and made possible a sharing of ideas, proposals for investigations and a gradual narrowing of focus. In the main this was achieved through newsletters and three conferences. The first of the latter was a launching conference to sketch out the major issues and set up a basic organization; the second was more theoretical and considered (1) the meaning of 'inner city', and (2) what insights might be derived from the existing literature; the third (in June 1977) examined work in progress which was presented in the form of research papers, reports and documentation. These papers are now being prepared for publication.

In September 1977 the Department of Education and Science made a small sum available to enable us to carry out a rapid investigation over a period of six months in order to discover the basic facts of linguistic diversity in inner-London schools, i.e. who speaks what? Incredible though it may seem, no reliable information is available on linguistic diversity in either the adult or the school population though the complexity of the picture in inner London is well known. The DES grant made it possible for one lecturer in the department and a half-time secretary to work on this investigation. It should be added that linguistic diversity, in its widest interpretation (i.e. to include all kinds of vernacular speech) is at the heart of many topics ripe for investigation. In fact, prior to the DES grant we had prepared 'Guidelines' for a do-it-yourself investigation by collaborating teachers and it provided a basis for our current work. The investigation has now been published as *Languages and Dialects of London Schoolchildren* (Rosen and Burgess 1981).

The survey has just completed its pilot stage in three schools, though the data have not yet been processed.

Here are some basic facts about the survey:

    i.   Population: all the first year pupils in 20 per cent of inner-London secondary schools.

   ii.   Report to be completed by end of current academic year.

  iii.   Two schools to be studied in depth; selected chiefly because of their participation in the wider project.

  iv.   Data to be collected:

       – numbers of pupils speaking a Great Britain based dialect (e.g. London, non-London, standard);

       – numbers of pupils speaking an overseas dialect of English;

       – numbers of pupils speaking a language other than English;

       – numbers of pupils speaking second languages and dialects, or third, fourth, etc. (i.e. different forms of bilingualism and bidialectalism);

       – teachers' estimates (3-point scale) of level of pupils' reading and writing of standard English.

1.2   While the survey has of necessity moved to the centre of our attention this year, other work has proceeded. Some of the varied undertakings that were reported at the June 1977 conference continue and others have been initiated. That variety of initiative is still fostered (e.g. a group working on writing by West Indian pupils, a study of language and use of television in science, etc.), but at the beginning of the current academic year the decision was taken to concentrate on two main themes. These are treated separately below.

The linguistic demands on the school (see section 2 below)

Our starting point is the Bullock Report's assertion that there is 'an indisputable gap'.

What exactly is 'the gap'? The guidelines suggest that there is a set of unexamined assumptions which stand behind the Report's assertion, and another set of underlying complicated issues that need to be laid bare. Above all we need to investigate what the 'linguistic demands' of schools, both implicit and explicit, actually are, assuming neither a consensus, nor obvious legitimation. We recognize that the undertaking of even the first steps in limited contexts bristles with difficulties. Nevertheless, we have set out a list of suggestions of starting points for individuals or small groups of collaborators and have outlined a specimen investigation. We have also tried to incorporate the notion that a study of 'linguistic demands' should include pupils' perceptions of these demands. Finally, we want to link all this to the setting of inner-city schools.

Language in collaborative learning (see section 3 below)

Teachers in inner-city schools are intensely aware that a continuation of methods that have been effective or appeared to be effective in other settings are unsuitable for their pupils. To put it differently, certain current ideas and practices recommend themselves strongly for trial, observation and deeper understanding. In particular among the participants in the project there is interest in the ways in which pupils can become participants in their own learning by working together in different ways. Some work is already afoot. The role of language in these contexts, therefore, suggests itself as a second focus for the project. As with the first, guidelines have been prepared for discussion at the January conference and they too set out some of the basic thinking and propose lines of work.

It can be seen that our undertaking has, in the course of a year and a half, moved through different phases, from a consciously open-ended approach that was hospitable to all possibilities through small investigations and reports ('work in progress'), to a very specific investigation (the survey) and two fresh initiatives (see sections 2 and 3 below).

2 Guidelines for Investigating the Linguistic Demands and Expectations of Schools in the Inner City

2.1 *Background*

For a year and a half a group of collaborators loosely linked together has been working on language in inner-city schools. The interests, styles of work and degrees of involvement have been diverse. Last June we held a conference at which a variety of discussion papers, documents and materials was put before the participants. These materials emerged from the work of teacher–researchers who had started from different places but were beginning to converge, or at least to start fitting together the jigsaw.

Out of the experience of previous work we felt we were ready to move the undertaking forward by selecting two themes for closer attention and to prepare guidelines that might be used by anyone who wished to work on them. This document then is meant to act as a guide for investigation of one of those themes.

Why be concerned about 'linguistic demands'?

It is perhaps worth saying that we are not very happy about the phrase and no doubt we shall find a better one. But it's also worth recalling how it wormed its way into our jargon. When we started we took the Bullock Report as a text (not Holy Writ!) in which we might find either valuable but undeveloped ideas and suggestions or unjustified, dubious, possibly muddled assumptions. Our combing of the text revealed, among other things, that at no point did the Report single out for separate careful scrutiny language in inner-city schools, though repeatedly it made references that clearly had them in mind. Amid these comments one stood out boldly: 'There is an indisputable gap between the language experiences that some families provide and the linguistic demands of school education' (para. 1.1.2).

We recognized this as a taking of sides in the debate that still rages about 'linguistic deprivation'. That debate we shall not pursue for the moment. For what is striking about the statement is that

i.   it assumes, or appears to, that there is a common set of 'linguistic demands' which all or most schools make of their pupils;

ii. it assumes that these demands are so well known that there is no need to spell them out, much less to indicate priorities or categories;

iii. it implies that these demands are all legitimate demands;

iv. it follows that, if pupils cannot meet these demands, the fault lies in them, their homes and their environment, rather than the possible inappropriateness of the demands.

In contrast we felt sure that

i.   linguistic demands varied greatly from school to school and even teacher to teacher (though probably there were some basic patterns; and the examination system was a great 'demander'). These differences are discussed in the opening pages of the

Bullock Report and Froome's 'Note of Dissent' at the end represents one extreme;

ii.   except for a few pious cover-all sentiments, e.g. that all children should be made literate, it is very difficult to know what exactly the demands are and what they mean; even explicit pro- grammes, declarations of intent, etc. do not really tell us what is actually happening;

iii. we needed to look critically at different kinds of demands and make some judgement of how justified they were;

iv.   we needed to look at the encounter between the pupil's estab- lished linguistic achievement (what he/she *can* do), and the demands the school makes on it (what he/she *should* do) in order to assess the effects of that encounter.

A tall order! But at least there was a clear starting point, a way in, for any teacher or small group of teachers. *What do we ask of our pupils?* The study might be made manageable by looking at, for example, a single pupil's experience, of a single aspect of language, say writing, or oral narrative.

A final point. We have already said that we are not too happy with the phrase 'linguistic demands' and explained how it's a legacy from the Bullock Report. We are dissatisfied with it for at least two reasons. First, it has an authoritarian ring about it that might easily lead us to exclude from our thinking such notions as encouragement, pupils and teacher creating possibilities and goals, pupil initiative, etc. In other words, the phrase might suggest that quite simply a pupil enters school and is confronted with a set of demands that he either meets or fails to meet. This is a much too artificial and simplified model. Secondly, the term does not really cover the richer notion of teacher aspiration, his hopes for his pupils and how they might together begin to formulate goals and routes, an interaction of expectations and aspirations.

Some underlying issues

A teacher may express 'a demand' of a most direct kind, such as – 'Each mistake in your composition must be corrected and the correct version written out three times'. Such demands are neither random nor whimsical but emerge from the teacher's formation, his educational philosophy, his response to his teaching experience, his reaction to pressures from parents, school policy, examinations, etc. Thus demands may be seen as expressing themselves in the day-to-day behaviour of teachers; but to understand them fully we need to see how the demand of the minute has behind it a whole 'nervous system' that threads its way through the educational system and society itself.

What we make explicit to ourselves about our practices of all kinds may differ dramatically from what we actually do. There is a strong folklore about this – 'practise what you preach'. So we may tell ourselves we are encouraging creativity when in practice we are teaching children to conform to an approved model. Conversely, we may think we are setting very limited goals (e.g. 'language skills') when in fact our teaching entails much more than that. In any case we all at some time or another have to acknowledge that our expectations were not met, not because they were in some way inappropriate but rather because something in the situation prevented this from happening. For these and other reasons any inquiry needs to look at both aspects of the language curriculum – how policy is formulated and articulated and how it emerges when pupils and teachers are engaged in day-to-day activities.

With the best will in the world, how the teacher perceives the situation and how the pupil perceives it may be very different, indeed they are likely to be so. It is never easy to capture the pupil's view but it is always worth attempting to do so.

We can never assume consistency. There are likely to be different, or even conflicting, demands within one school, one department or one teacher. This may not be so simple a matter as inconsistency. Flexibility may come into it and over a period of time there are changes that arise from experience.

Obviously the demands of the school now need to be discussed in the context of the current debate about standards ('back to basics', etc.). How does a school (1) set its standards (2) achieve them?

Explicit policy

In what sense can we say a school makes linguistic demands? Clearly there are many ways in which pupils receive very direct messages that there are expectations, attitudes and, sometimes, firm insistence that their language should be used in certain kinds of ways and that it should conform to instruction, advice or more general principles. We might consider the channels through which those promptings might come:

  i.   the English teachers and the English department;
 ii.   any other teachers;
iii.   more general school-wide channels, e.g. a language policy across the curriculum, a statement by the head, etc.

It seems likely that pupils have to accumulate and 'read' ever explicit policy, make some attempt to put it together coherently. Even a coherent presentation will not tell them everything.

Let's consider then some of the ways in which explicit policy might reach them:

   i.   efforts to change their speech;

   ii.   efforts to teach directly standard English in writing, possibly with high or low priority given to spelling, punctuation and 'mechanics';

   iii.   the organization of discussions, groups, etc. with the explicit goals of developing discussion skills;

   iv.   the availability of certain kinds of books and claims about their value (possibly the dismissing of others);

   v.   the teaching of writing skills, e.g. the teacher might offer advice about planning, organization of the text, stylistic precepts, etc.;

   vi.   there might be the inculcation of certain values, e.g. honesty, sincerity, precision, etc. or a general attitude stated ('I prefer plain straightforward English');

   vii.   a specific cognitive demand in the form that certain uses of language will foster certain kinds of thinking;

   viii.   language specific to certain subjects might be insisted on: this may consist of little more than the use of technical terms but is likely to extend to format of notes, reports, etc.

It may be that some curriculum areas are more demanding and language-conscious than others. Some may give more salience to the spoken language rather than the written or vice versa. It may well be that language demands are very capricious in the sense that they depend almost entirely on the attitudes and goals of individual teachers. But isn't there likely to be a prevailing pattern or patterns? There are also more general channels, i.e. critical occasions in school life when a school-wide linguistic demand is made, e.g. to conform to examination demands, real or supposed; to use certain forms of address (sir, madam); advice on how to talk to visitors; perhaps even documents that are circulated. The most elaborate school-wide demand is likely to figure in a language-across-the-curriculum policy but these are few and far between.

Implicit demands

Most school pupils change their spoken language within the school context. It seems likely that this is due not so much to direct teaching as forces that operate very obliquely. How do they work? The ways in which it has been suggested that more or less direct intervention operate could all be converted into indirect ways. In any case there is

no hard and fast dividing line. This could all do with careful exploration for obviously it could be the common core of the hidden curriculum
or part of it. Once again the pupils' perceptions of what is going on
must be of great significance, e.g. of the speaking roles allocated in class
lessons, or of the various models presented by the language of teachers.

The inner city

What we have discussed so far might be true of any school anywhere.
What is there about our theme that might be of particular relevance in
inner-city schools? We criticized the Bullock Report's statement but
there is this much to it. All those who have taught in inner-city schools
are likely to agree that the traditional language expectations and
activities need at least some reshaping, if not radical reconsideration in
that context. First, the whole fabric of the inner-city communities has
changed and is changing. That by itself means that the linguistic
community is changing. A largely shared London vernacular has given
way to diversification of dialects and languages. Pupils for whom
English is a second language are numerous. How are teachers to work
with pupils who use some kind of 'inter-language' – e.g. are at some
stage between a mother tongue language/dialect and the target
language adopted by school? Parental expectations, including of course
language expectations, have changed and are likely to be articulated
more forcibly.

The harsh facts of unemployment are likely to push those expectations in particular directions. The notorious effects of inner-urban decay
are more likely to subject the demands of the school to ruthless scrutiny
from outside. In this setting teachers are more likely to be sharply
divided about the special needs of pupils and in their attitudes to
cultural diversity; many will occupy a middle ground.

In general we may ask: In what ways are the linguistic demands of
the school appropriate to the inner-city context? What can and do
schools offer to immigrant language learners, indigenous speakers of
minority varieties of English (including Creole and local varieties)?
What do schools need to do to encourage the diverse speakers to use
English in motivated ways?

2.2   Ways of working

The importance of the context

While our focus is on language, we cannot 'inspect' the abstractions
(demands and expectations) separately from the climate of learning,
the kinds of activities that are given priority, what pupils are

encouraged to do, what they initiate, etc. In other words our central concern is embedded in the kinds of learning and teaching that are being fostered.

It follows then that a sensitive description and observation of life in the class-room must be the solid foundation on which more focused investigation must be built.

These notes are intended to serve as a basis on which any of us wishing to start work on this area of the research might get started. We are trying to follow the principle we have repeatedly stressed – that suggestions should take a form which enables even the most modest and limited investigation to get under way and at the same time makes provision for more ambitious inquiries to take place.

We suggest that the first decision to be made is which of two approaches is preferred. The decision will turn on several criteria – practicalities of the school situation, present interests and activities, etc., though probably in the end it may amount to a personal preference. We see the two approaches in this way.

1   *Narrow focus*   The strategy here is to look at *a single language activity*, bearing in mind that other activities, both linguistic and broadly educational, will be involved.

2   *Broad focus*   With this approach the intention is to look at all language activities (once again in context) as they interact and complement each other.

Suggestions for working with narrow focus

Possible areas: kinds of reading, kinds of writing, kinds of talk, the language of the teacher (written and spoken), the reading and writing of non-fiction, the language of worksheets, 'mechanics' (spelling, punctuation, etc.), carry-over from dialects and languages, oral narrative, language in drama, etc.

Our suggestions will show that 'narrowness' is a flexible term and implies that some valuable study is needed on very specific questions, some of which will seem narrower than others.

Specimen topic – narrow approach: We set out below a sketch of how one possible topic might be worked on, the topic being 'Kinds of Reading'. It clearly cannot be regarded as a model because each will need its own approach, but it is meant to illustrate the possibilities.

Kinds of Reading

Aim: To discover what demands and possibilities are generated in the school and how pupils are helped to respond to them.

Collecting and recording:
  i. Collect a dossier (photocopies or page numbers where photo-copying is not practical) of reading demands in
         a child's day/week
         a teacher's day/week
         a class for each of the years in a school.
  ii. Description of the contexts (or at least some of them) in which the items in i. occur.
  iii. Who is having difficulty and why? Or positively, who can take on the task and why? This might be dealt with very explicitly, e.g. one pupil: what can he/she cope with? What can he/she not cope with?

Discussion and analysis: The next stage is interpreting the material collected, formulating hypotheses or questions, tentative conclusions, comparisons with material from other inquiries, and formulating the next stage (if any). This is the point at which the work needs to be more closely linked with the whole research enterprise (e.g. material prepared for general discussion and, possibly, dissemination).

Suggestions for working with broad focus
Is there a document articulating the school's intentions and aspirations relating to aspects of language throughout the school? How far is this an instrument of realized policy and how far is it a guide for the future?

Is there an English Department document akin to a language policy document? (A syllabus? Open records of staff discussions? Advice to new teachers, etc.?)

Do any other departments lay down explicit recommendations on linguistic matters? Are there textbooks or courses to which pupils are expected to devote considerable attention?

Finally, how much can be *inferred* from any documents?

At this point it is worth stressing that in no sense can the inspection of documents of the kind referred to be clandestine. *It can only be carried out with the co-operation of the teachers involved.*

An examination of the documents should have as its aim a laying bare of the principles that are expressed or implied by them. Some of them may have done this already. It should be a preliminary to a study of how much they coincide with or differ from what is attempted in the class-room. They can also reveal fundamental attitudes and aspirations of the school or a department or a group of collaborating teachers. It is likely, for example, that a group of teachers engaged in initiating and developing integrated work will set down their starting points and plans.

Observation and recording: To show the range and variety of ways in which pupils are expected to function. For this purpose colleagues will certainly need to collaborate, taking it in turns to take on the task of observer. We suggest a start might be made with one or more of these objectives in mind:

   i.   a day's or week's experience with a class;
   ii.   a day or week with a teacher;
   iii.   a cross-section (day? week?) obtained by looking at one class from each of years 1–5.

What should be recorded? And how should it be recorded?
There are, of course, standard observation schedules (headings under which 'events' are classified). There are several weaknesses to this system but, for our purposes, the greatest of them is that they discourage teachers from observing freely and evolving their own category systems. Recording should include:

- the style of working (small groups; one 'task' or different 'tasks'; carry-over across weeks or months; teacher's role, etc.).
- what precisely are pupils asked to do; what do they think they have been asked to do?
- what materials are involved?
- what do the pupils do?
- what does the teacher do while they're doing it?

More specifically about language:

- when, if at all, does the teacher make explicit language 'demands' and what are they? (E.g. 'Tell this story in your own words'.)
- when, if at all, do pupils raise language questions? (E.g. 'Can you say . . . ?')
- do certain *attitudes* to language emerge? (E.g. of a vernacular idiom 'That's an interesting expression; what does it mean?')
- what levels of expectation are implied by the written and printed materials available?
- what does the teaching style imply? (E.g. does the organization of the work suggest that pupils are expected to talk to reach understanding?)

–how is linguistic/cultural diversity handled?

–what happens to pupils who are having difficulty part or all of which can be said to be a language difficulty? (E.g. they cannot understand the language of the worksheet.)

Some topics for discussion:

i.   What kind of relationship is there between the demands and the responses of the pupils? (A match? A mismatch? A bit of both?)

ii. What is the relationship between the demands as they emerge in the class-room and declared policy (syllabus, etc.)?

iii. Is there a clear-cut patterning among the pupils, i.e. Which pupils respond well to which demands? Any differences of sex? Ethnic groups?

iv. How have the pupils perceived it all?

v.   What does a first set of observations suggest needs looking at more closely?

2.3   Developing the work

We hope that enough of us will have carried out work along the lines suggested to be able to pool ideas, let us say, by Easter. We shall need to formulate them in a way that would be helpful to any teachers who had not participated in the investigation. We should be able to suggest a next stage in the inquiry.

3   Language and Collaborative Learning

3.1   The purpose of this paper is to invite your participation in a study of language and collaborative learning in school.

We explain more fully what we mean by this later. As a rough indication for now, we are interested in the mutual support that pupils can give to each others' learning, whether through informal or more formally organized collaboration in class-room activities.

At present there is relatively little systematic documentation and analysis of such ways of working; and virtually none that takes as its especial focus the language of the range of learning contexts in which pupil collaboration can occur. We should also like to work towards a more detailed understanding of the value of collaborative work in school. We believe that there is already evidence to indicate that it has considerable potential.

This investigation is one strand within a larger undertaking concerned with language and inner-city schools. Our way of working on this ha itself been collaborative. Teachers, lecturers, researchers, various institutions within the ILEA have all been contributors. We are seeking to open a dialogue, a working dialogue, through exchange of papers and through regular conferences.

Our way of seeking your help in this paper reflects this background. Any contribution that you feel able to make, however small, would be welcome. We want to allow any more systematic view to emerge from what people feel able to contribute. And at the same time we are asking you to join in the dialogue more generally if you feel able to.

In the remainder of this paper we set out in more detail what we mean by collaborative learning and make some suggestions for things that you might do to help take the thinking about this further. If you are interested in contributing, the procedure is simple. Contact us. Alternatively, make a start with one of the suggestions and then get in touch.

An initial hypothesis is that the support that pupils are able to give to each others' learning may be critical to achievement in inner-city class-rooms.

Shared pupil talk is one aspect of such collaboration that has been extensively considered in recent years. You'll be familiar with the Bullock Report's emphasis on this. In talking things over the pupils' understandings may be refined by the pressure on formulation and reformulation. The following snatch of conversation between two 11-year-olds provides an example.

A　People who are cremated are just famous people.
B　No they ain't.
A　Yes.
B　No.
B　My old grandad was cremated . . . just buried in the sea.
A　But still . . . Drake was buried in the sea.
B　Well he [grandfather] weren't famous . . . well then.
A　He was famous to your family though.
B　You don't have to be famous to be buried though.
A　Well then . . . see . . . I told you.
B　And you don't have to be famous to be cremated.

Here an initial disagreement draws itself up into a spirited battle of wits, which allows both pupils (A and B) to articulate features of their understandings about burial and cremation. Their conceptions are still at a fairly rudimentary stage. Yet perhaps it is through the support that they give to each other in conversations such as these, and as importantly through the habit of talking, that development towards more precise concepts may be fostered.

Taking such talk as one example of collaboration in learning we should like to know more generally:

* whether the quality of what pupils achieve individually is dependent in part on the collaboration that permeates the class-room more widely;
* whether collaboration between pupils in different aspects of curriculum learning enables them to get further than they might have been able to achieve on their own;
* to what extent it may be possible to reorder aspects of curriculum learning which are commonly approached on an individualized basis so as to make available the potential of collaborative learning;
* how the conditions for collaborative learning may be established (and what the constraints on it are in school); for example, how tolerances and expectations are developed among the pupils;
* how different dimensions in the way in which collaborative learning situations are organized affect the performance of pupils within them. Later, we suggest some of the dimensions in which we are interested.

Evidence gathered along the lines of these questions would, we believe, have important implications for the organization of learning in inner-city class-rooms. For example, the snatch of conversation above derives from a longer simulation-cum-drama-cum-debate (no other term will do) which one teacher used as a way of encouraging a more explicit and focused collaboration between her pupils, with the intention of deepening their understandings about beliefs and burial customs in other societies. Clearly, it would have been possible to have developed these themes either in less focused or more individualized ways – through class-room instruction, for instance, or through reading or through worksheet questions. A stress on collaboration raises an area of delicate choice for the teacher and the need for an understanding of the alternatives within which such choices may be made.

Our request to you in this is straightforward. It is through documentation and analysis of collaboration across a range of contexts that we are most likely to arrive at a comprehensive picture. We feel fairly sure that in many class-rooms there are ways of encouraging pupils' support for each others' learning which are not yet widely articulated. A pooling, by which the areas from among which the teacher draws his choice may be expanded, is one objective for the study. Equally, what is needed in analysis is a discussion that is sensitive to long-term organizations in the class-room and to the long-term histories of interaction of the pupils in it. This is something that only the teacher in the class-room can finally supply.

We appreciate that the time that you may have to give to this may not be great. So we have tried to graduate the ways in which you might contribute. What would help above all would be the provision of documentation and examples to enable us to add to our picture of the range of learning contexts in which pupil collaboration occurs. If you were able to add to this some analysis, that of course would be doubly helpful. This might include an indication of the balance between those points at which you make specific provision for the interaction of pupils in common tasks and those learnings where you leave pupils (and expect them) to achieve on their own. Beyond this lie more subtle assumptions. It seems likely that the co-operation which pupils can achieve in *explicitly* organized moments of class-room learning is dependent itself on understandings which are more *implicitly* fostered as part of the ongoing organization of the class-room. If you have feelings about these in your own teaching, clearly it would help to know about them.

One or two last points will help narrow the focus. In principle we assume that collaborative working is tied to no particular area of the curriculum. Yet we recognize that there may be differences between subjects over this and think it would be worth while to explore them. Of particular interest here would be to develop a sense of the various contexts of learning in different curriculum subjects, in which individualized or collaborative learning was felt to be appropriate.

We have assumed for the most part that you will wish to make your contribution to this investigation on an individual basis. Yet we are also hopeful that some examination of this kind might become a focus for a group of staff together in the context of thinking about language across the curriculum. Needless to say we would be especially interested in any comparisons that you might be able to draw between different teaching styles or in any conclusions that you may come to collectively.

Our specific interest, as we have already said, is in the possibilities of collaborative learning within the inner-city class-room. We do not wish to inhibit contributions from other contexts, but it is right to make that central concentration clear. What is especially characteristic of the inner-city class-room is the linguistic diversity among the pupils who compose it. Thus we have a special interest in those contexts where pupils are coming together from bases in different dialects of English and different mother tongues.

In a companion paper to this we are attempting to launch, on a similar basis, a study of the language demands of the school. It may be helpful to see our most general hope in this study from this angle. Emphases within school on collaboration or on individualized learning are, from one perspective, a component of the language demands, implicitly signalled. Our interest in the collaborative organization of learning derives from the hunch that this may be a critical way forward within the diversity of the inner-city class-room.

3.2 *Notes towards the study of language in collaborative learning*

We want to set out here some notes that will be helpful in enabling you to begin a more systematic look at collaborative learning. To attempt to be comprehensive would be unwise. So we hope that you will take our suggestions as indications of possible lines rather than exact specifications. In effect, we suggest three areas of interest in collaborative learning, with some suggestions for points of entry into these areas and suggestions for what these points of entry might include; and with some suggestions too for variations in focus from the broadly comprehensive to the more narrowly focused. None of this is meant to prevent other points of entry, of course, or other responses. We are offering an outline only.

3.2.1 *The interrelation of individualized and collaborative work*
This would be to contribute to the general picture about those kinds of learning that are typically left to pupils to achieve on their own and those where the support of other pupils is typically involved. We are conscious that the contrast is forced. It is a flow of class-room activity that is typical. We are drawing lines for the purpose of analysis. This area of interest, though, could be a good place to begin, because the analysis that you build up here could serve as a basis for moving out to later suggestions.

Point of entry: Analysis in your own teaching over a period (or with a group of colleagues) of those points where you allow for pupils to support each others' learning and ways in which collaboration is fostered.

What the study might include: Analysis of a class's work over a week.
  i. Broad indication of sequences of lesson content and class activity.
 ii. Variations in class basis of activity (describe or tabulate these).
     For example:
     – Whole class collectively
     – Groups with a focused project
     – Pairs with a focused project

- Individualized work with the possibility of collaboration
- Individualized work without the possibility of collaboration

iii.   Indication of role of teacher in relation to these activities.

iv.   Selection by observation of significant points of collaboration.
- those that have been formally organized by you
- informal: those that the pupils set in motion on their own

v.   Relation of these to your perception of longer term patterns of collaboration within the class, e.g.:
- priorities that you attempt specifically to foster
- patterns of interaction within the class – who works with whom.

vi.   More general commentary, analysis and evaluation.

Variations in focus: We have suggested a whole class for a week. But it would be possible to vary the focus both as to the periods of time and the whole class basis – for example, a group of pupils only, or even a single pupil, or one or two pupils selected for special reasons. And again, not for a whole week, but for a single period or more, or for a self-contained sequence of work.

3.2.2   *Exploration of possibilities of reordering normally individualized learning as collaborative*

This would be to contribute to a picture of the range of learning contexts in which pupils can work collaboratively. We make three suggestions below. These may well seem rather familiar to you if you are working this way already. What we are seeking though is documentation and, if possible, your evaluation of this way of working. Also the suggestions are intended only to be indicative. We would be just as interested in other forms of collaborative working – on a smaller or, if you like, a larger scale. Probably the main danger that we run in attempting to compile this picture of the range of contexts is that of losing touch with reality. It is not what would be nice to do that we are after, but what is practicable.

Point of entry: Analysis of one (or more) experimental attempt to substitute a collaborative basis for a learning task which is normally handled through individualized learning.

What the study might include: three examples

Substitution of working groups for (e.g.) whole class teaching or (e.g.) individualized worksheet writing.

i.   Description of topic and associated learning envisaged.

ii.   Description of organization of working situation:
      − Task set
      − Composition of groups (etc.)
iii. Indication of role of teacher in relation to the activities.
iv.   Selective documentation of working groups − (e.g.) tapes, end products, etc.
v.   Relation of collaborative achievement to other patterns of achievement within the class and to underlying patterns of collaboration between pupils.
vi.   Any more general commentary, analysis and evaluation.

Variations in focus: Similar considerations apply to those in 3.2.1 above. Probably to attempt to document the working of a whole class will be an excessive labour. We should be as interested in examination of a group of pupils or one or two pupils selected for special reasons. Clearly the time envisaged is variable too, ranging from a single period to an extended sequence of learning.

Other suggestions within this area of interest: It is not necessary to repeat for these suggestions the kind of framework suggested in (i–vi) above the substitution of working groups. That framework applies without significant alterations to the suggestions below. Almost certainly you will be able to think of other examples of collaboration that would be worth documenting.

2 Reading
   For example − collaborative first reading of a passage or text
                − a small group interpretation, with or without the teacher's assistance
                − a group production arising out of reading
                − retrospective discussion in pairs or groups about materials encountered

3 Writing
   For example − a collaborative drafting (e.g.) of story, photoplay, report
                − collaborative working at one stage of the writing process (e.g.) at first draft stage, at final draft stage on the basis of individual drafts
                − retrospective discussion in pairs or groups about pieces of written work

Variations of focus: Similar considerations apply to those entered above.

3.2.3   *Analysis of contextual dimensions affecting collaborative learning*

This would be to contribute to our understanding of the range of factors affecting the nature and quality of collaborative learning in different situations. One factor in this, clearly enough, is the nature of the topic, the task set, the associated learning envisaged. As well as this, though, it seems possible to disentangle a variety usually interwoven in specific situations, which it would be useful to understand more fully. We suggest our own list of these below. There may be others. In suggesting this as a specific area of interest we do not mean to imply that these threads are not also relevant in our earlier suggestions. We separate them here for convenience of presentation. Our assumption is that it will be helpful to suggest discrete focuses, even though in the end the areas are not wholly separable.

Point of entry: Organization of a sequence of learning with some collaborative basis and with one of the following contextual dimensions in mind.

What the study might include: Documentation and analysis of the learning of the group.

Possible dimensions

(1)   The teacher's role: this is too subtle and variable for any simple range of alternative possibilities to be presented. There is some sort of scale from dominance to withdrawal and it would be interesting to compare the performance of groups with or without the teacher present. But there are many other points of interest. In collaborative situations how are the responsibilities dispersed between teacher and pupils? Where does control lie? Who facilitates the contributions of group members? Who concretizes and who abstracts? How is the value of the group's work reflected back to them?

(2)   The pupil's expectations: ideally one would study this developmentally. We envisage here a concentration on how pupils construe and interpret the demands of collaborative work. How do they perceive its value? How do they perceive and respond to the demands made on them? What is the place for retrospective reflection on activity? Potentially this seems one of the most significant points of analysis but one that is only likely to yield substantial insight against the background of relatively sustained experience of collaborative working. It would be useful too to consider not only how pupils perceive the value of collaborative working but where also they perceive its limits.

(3)   Constraints within the task set: the potential range is daunting. We suggest just one or two possibilities below. These suggestions are to some extent motivated by the common feeling that pupils need to develop the capacity to deal with more open tasks via proceeding from the more narrowly focused ones. It would be useful to have some consideration of this.

No end point for group	....	With end point
		(e.g. a production, a discussion)
'Discussion'	....	Drama
'Discussion' as focus	....	Activity as focus
		(e.g. preparing display)
Free roles	....	Assigned roles
		(e.g. 'You argue for this')

(4)   Size and composition of group: these are separable considerations. How language and performance vary according to size of group is one thread. Of more powerful interest probably is the way in which the group is composed. How does the productivity (usefulness) of the group relate to the separate contributions of its members? What is the inter-relation of topic and task set with the separate interests, expertise and experience of the individuals involved?

The well-known gap between presentation and publication means that intervening events make what was originally said not quite what would be said today. We stand by the ideas expressed here but the 'Language in Inner-city Schools' Project has changed. It's worth mentioning two lengthy reports of conferences held during 1981. The first was called *Achieving Literacy* and the second, organised as a joint endeavour with the School Council 'Language for Learning' Project was called *Investigating Talk*.

2

Language Teaching Research
and Its Effect on Teachers in Early Education

HAZEL FRANCIS

Introduction

An attempt to evaluate recent research into language teaching in early education, in the space of a paper of this length, necessarily entails a simplification of the picture and a selection of aspects that seem to me to be worth discussion. I shall initially simplify by pointing to two conceptions of language teaching that are important to teachers and are evident in the research literature. One is that of special, separate language teaching, and the other is that of language teaching and learning as an integral feature of early school experience. These two conceptions are to be found whether one looks at intervention programmes or at more general research into language in the nursery and primary sector. Since much recent research has centred on the idea of intervention, most of my review, but not all, will select features from this work. I shall select with four discussion points in mind – the problem of appropriate evaluation of language teaching, the issue of the relationship between language and other skills at both the theoretical and practical levels, the question of the nature of any educationally incapacitating language deficit or difference, and the problem of defining what aspect of language is to be developed, especially when attention shifts from form to function. After reviewing and discussing selected research, I shall move to the question of its impact on teachers in the research projects and in a selection of nursery and primary schools.

Review of Research

Bereiter and Engelmann (1966) influenced the development of special language intervention programmes with their statement to the effect that disadvantaged children had special language training needs, which more of the traditional nursery kind of education could not satisfy. Programmes like theirs, or like that of Blank and Solomon (1968), have not been developed in this country; but intervention projects, emphasizing language skills, have certainly been explored. When Bernstein's thesis, that aspects of their language learning put lower working-class children at an educational disadvantage, coincided with an increase in our schools in the numbers of immigrant children of non-English speaking origins, we joined our transatlantic cousins in considering ways of meeting the needs of such disadvantaged and minority group children.

Notions of compensatory education have meant that much research has been implemented through nursery schools or playgroups rather than through the home or through the primary school, though follow-up has sometimes continued into the compulsory school years. Nursery school work meant two sources of confusion in interpreting gain scores for children in intervention programmes. One was the difficulty of operating a particular teaching programme without at the same time necessarily introducing features of nursery schooling in general, and the other was that of knowing on what basis of parental policy or practice children had been subjected to nursery programmes. Whether gain scores were interpreted within a programme, or in a comparison between a programme and a control group, the difficulty was still present. Given that programmes could differ among themselves, and that the actors and scenario in their implementation could also vary considerably, perhaps it was not to be wondered at that the Westinghouse Evaluation of Headstart schemes in America reported little if anything to show in the way of benefit by the time children were established in grade schooling. Nevertheless individual well-controlled studies that did suggest value in intervention programmes could be found.

British studies have in fact been small scale; but, because they followed quickly on American work, they have sometimes made use of ideas or programmes specifically worked out in the United States. Following the Plowden recommendations of 1967, amounting to positive discrimination to bring disadvantaged children to the same position as advantaged at the start of the educational race, the DES promoted the EPA (Educational Priority Area) development and research outlined in the Halsey Report of 1972 and developed more fully in a subsequent series of reports. The general concept behind these programmes was what came to be called 'action research' – the evaluation of the effect of intervening in and changing some aspect of education. In fact, th research seemed to try to cover both programme comparisons and the effects of particular interventions, and included much beginning and end state measurement as well as ongoing checking on the implementation of projects. The place of language teaching and learning in these programmes can only be worked out by teasing it from reports that contain many other features of intervention in early education. I shall not attempt to cover all the ground in the Halsey series, but I shall select from it after I have used two other studies that were more clearly language intervention projects.

An earlier study (Gahagan and Gahagan 1970) reported what was essentially a language training programme. It derived directly from the early Bernstein thesis and, mindful of the problems of nursery school comparisons, compared an 'experimental' group with control groups of children drawn from several primary schools. For the experimental group a great deal of work went into translating into practice the aim of fostering the teachers' encouragement of children's talking – in comment on ongoing activity and in question and explanation. This was seen to be what the 'ideal teacher' does, but what is hard to achieve in practice. What teachers found helpful were very practical suggestions about verbal games, physical means of concentrating children's attention on listening (listening in the dark, listening through telephone receivers, wearing masks, etc.), sets of picture materials designed to foster different kinds of language use and suggestions about the use of drama. What was actually done in the project was to structure the use of these activities according to specific language aims to do with improving auditory discrimination, attention, span of attention and varied comprehension and production skills.

What is difficult to estimate is the usefulness of the researchers' evaluation technique. They used an experimental design incorporating a 'Hawthorne effect' control group and a 'no treatment' control group, and compared pre-test and post-test scores on a variety of tests. Ostensibly the differences in favour of the experimental group were attributed to the effect of the twenty minutes per day devoted by the teachers to the experimental treatment. It is difficult, however, to be convinced that the 'treatment' did not have effects on the whole teaching/learning situation throughout the school day, affecting both the ways teachers acted and the ways pupils expected them to act. Indeed, the authors were explicitly hoping to achieve such a spread of effect; but without some reporting of what actually happened in the nursery classes *before* the treatment, during the treatment periods, and during the rest of the nursery day, it is difficult to know how far change was due to some indirect effect through training 'trainable' teachers, rather than to a direct and specific set of effects of the programme on the children.

A further problem, of which the authors were well aware, lay in defining and measuring features of language development other than certain aspects of vocabulary. They wrote as if, had the right kind of standardized measures been available, the relationship of 'treatment' to theory and to measurement would have resulted in a better evaluation. It is this hope in their approach that I shall consider more seriously when I come to the questions of theoretical distinctions and of the nature of supposed language deficit and difference. Suffice it to say here that I do not think the 'experimental' type of evaluation can survive the questions. It would, of course, be important that standardized measures were used if the treatment were intended to ameliorate a measurable deficit or difference. It would also, and here the literature shows gaps, be important to see what effects the treatment had on the supposedly advantaged. If it were equally powerful, that would call in question a model of deficit that implies that middle-class children's experience takes them to ceiling levels in development. The next project I have selected did in fact attempt this question.

The NFER-sponsored Pre-school Project (reported very clearly by Martin Woodhead 1976 a and b) was a classically designed comparison between a treatment and a control group, intended to investigate effects of special language and perceptual programmes. It suffered many of the defects of such an evaluation applied to educational contexts – defects arising from the inability to allocate children randomly to treatment groups, the necessity of using different versions of tests to suit pre-test and post-test age ranges, and the difficulty or impossibility of controlling extraneous variables such as amount of schooling and home background and family features. Rather than dwell on the finer criticism of design and statistics, I am inclined to interpret the findings as showing more favourable gains in the 'experimental' group and on language measures in particular. Yet, as Woodhead comments, it is difficult to relate the abilities tested (the relevant language measures used were the EPVT and the ITPA scales) either to the preliminary notion of deficit or to the nature of the programme. Moreover, when the effects of length of programme experience were explored it appeared that (with the qualification that age was a confounded variable) two terms were better than one; but that, contrary to expectations, continued work with 'Peabody' after this period did not result in continued 'compensation' effects. Woodhead commented that this was in line with certain American studies where the variables were better controlled. He also pointed out that there seems to be no ready way of assessing whether beginning the programme at three years or four years is the better approach, since there is no analysis of differential age suitability. In so far as the question has been explored in the United States there is no conclusive finding either way.

This project, incorporating in its nursery groups children from all social classes, allowed the questions of pre-existing differences and differential treatment effects to be explored. The language pre-test scores, unlike the perceptual pre-test scores, showed what we have come to expect in the way of many language test differences between social classes, but the treatment effects were *similar for all classes*. Deficit was not made up through treatment – all children benefited.

But we are still left asking about the nature of this benefit, especially since it appeared to be optimal after a relatively short period of treatment – and the more so since a follow-up study into the primary school years indicated a 'wash-out' of effects, and no difference between treatment and control group children in attainment in arithmetic and reading, nor in general behavioural measures. In his final chapter, Woodhead suggests one possible answer – that the Peabody programme is actually a *way of teaching the appropriate techniques* for the language tests used. Now the NFER evaluation procedure could not inform us on this point. Some other evaluation analysis might – but it suggests that a searching probe into what actually goes on in language teaching and in testing is required. This is a similar conclusion to one I made from looking at the Gahagan study.

The DES and SSRC sponsored work in Educational Priority Areas, reported by Halsey and his colleagues, included a variety of intervention programmes. They were concentrated into a three-year 'action research' programme in four areas – the West Riding, Birmingham, Deptford and Liverpool. There was a further project sponsored by the Scottish Education Department and the SSRC in Dundee. As Halsey pointed out in his introduction to the third volume of the reports (Barnes 1975), each project experienced a unique combination of teacher action and philosophy, local educational practice and values, and social and economic background. Thus the projects developed different interventions and different approaches to evaluation, but all suffered the difficulty of describing educational and social action in terms of measured outcomes. The nature and place of language teaching has to be teased out of each project. Some expected it to affect tested language skills, some expected it to affect other aspects of development, and others expected other teaching to affect language skill. It was intended that special language teaching should find a place in all the projects, and that the Peabody Language Development Kit should be used; but teachers', advisers' and administrators' reactions to the programme resulted in various modifications.

I do not think it would be particularly helpful to press the analysis into too much detail, so the Birmingham, West Riding and Liverpool projects are grouped together. Here the teachers were willing to give the Peabody Kit a try; and, with various modifications, it was used in playgroups and nursery schools. Groups using it were variously compared with control groups, and with groups using respectively a modified individual programme in the style of Marion Blank's (West Riding), another language programme 'Wotever Next' (Liverpool) and a number programme (Birmingham). The results were marginally in favour of the experimental groups over the controls with respect to measures on the English Picture Vocabulary Test and the Reynell Language Development Scale; but little can be made of this, and the same questions as in other studies arise about the relationship of deficit or difference to the programme, and of both to the tests. What kind of learning was actually going on and how? Halsey commented that the results suggested that whether the programme made any difference to language scores depended on the quality of the general teaching in the nursery or school. In very good nursery schools it appeared to make no difference.

Two rather different stories of intervention came from Deptford and Dundee, where teachers were much more involved in working out its nature, and the outcome was clearly more a case of curriculum development than one of experimental treatment. In Deptford, the nursery teachers felt that their training and equipment were such that the Peabody Kit was neither in harmony with their practice nor useful as a teaching material. They decided instead to develop a programme of intensifying language teaching through short sessions of ordinary nursery play activity in small groups, but this eventually worked out as one-to-one interaction between a teacher and a child within the ordinary class-room activities. Evaluation then included the documenting of those activities that facilitated such one-to-one interaction, and recording of verbal exchanges in order to analyse the teachers' implementation of the intervention strategy. It was possible to compare intervention class-rooms with controls, and target children with controls *within* the 'experimental' class-rooms. The EPVT and Reynell Scales were used as pre- and post-test measures of the children's language skills, and observation schedules were filled in to give a basis for comparison of amount of time spent in verbal exchange in various 'play' contexts. Here we are getting nearer the question of what is actually happening, but no nearer to relating the verbal interaction to the language measures used. It is perhaps not surprising then to discover that the 'experimental' and control children did not differ – but there was a general improvement in scores both within and between class-rooms. Nevertheless there was some change observed in the ways teachers managed their class-rooms to achieve more one-to-one interaction.

Also in Deptford certain work had begun in the EPA junior schools before the nursery project developed, and continued after it had finished. This work was aimed to gear the curriculum towards the perceived spoken language needs of EPA children. Initial ideas were to help teachers to see these needs as centred in 'verbalizing about their experience', and to encourage them to saturate the school work with readings from literature. Various materials and techniques were developed in co-operation with the teachers, and during the first year teachers were interviewed to assess how work was developing. Their reactions resulted in the formation of regular discussion groups to clarify what it was all about, rather than to become too engrossed in the detail of technique and in modification of class-room work. In the second year, when nine teachers were attempting to develop this curriculum change, the researchers found it increasingly difficult to define their role. They were being drawn in to teacher-training and class-room management roles that they had not anticipated, and for which they had neither previous experience not the 'in-group' language. They were unhappily aware that often their assessment of what was happening could be no more than acceptance of the teacher's reports. As to assessing the effects on the children's language, they were in no better a position than other researchers, who used control groups and EPVT and ITPA scores. The outcome was difficult to weigh up because of variance control problems, and there was no real sign of effect from the curriculum development.

The Dundee experiment in intervention was one of curriculum development involving nursery school teachers, but it emphasized concept rather than language development. A structured concept syllabus was worked out and teachers were encouraged to develop it in terms of series or 'themes', of daily small group activities called 'playsems'. In these the children were to use the play materials, songs and stories that the teacher felt to be best and most opportune in their own settings. These were to be the means of fostering the growth of the relevant concepts. The syllabus eventually included 227 'playsems' grouped into fifty-one themes, and lasted over something like two years. Continued review and discussion guided the development of both what was to be taught and how records were to be kept. One guesses that teachers' records of individual children's activities might be a fruitful source of evaluation information, but I have found no reference to its being used. Instead, an end-state evaluation of the work is reported, in which children receiving the teaching were compared with controls in both the same schools and in other non-intervention schools. Measures were obtained on the EPVT and the Reynell Scale and on sub-tests of the Weschler Intelligence Scale (WIPPSI). There was no clear advantage to the children in the 'playsem' groups, but a fairly consistent balance in their favour. Nevertheless, there were considerable improvements in scores for all children undergoing nursery education, and the researchers were inclined to attend to this evidence of the over-all advantage of nursery provision rather than to finer points of difference between kinds of provision. Perhaps in a context where such an impressively well-structured programme as the 'playsem' approach could be worked out, the standard of nursery teaching was already very high. As with Deptford then, we are left with a wish that more had been reported about the processes of teaching and learning, but we are *not* asked to see intervention as specifically aimed to foster language development, we are much clearer about the structure of intervention, and we see aims of the curriculum being related to the range of language and cognitive tests used in the evaluation. In these respects the project stands on its own.

My comments on research into language teaching of a non-intervention kind will be more brief. I shall again be selective rather than comprehensive, and shall take two projects to illustrate the issues I wish to raise.

The first is that reported by Connie and Harold Rosen as the 1969–71 Schools Council Project on Language Development in the Primary School (Rosen and Rosen 1973). The main aim was to show the range of language used by children in the 5- to 11-year age range and to give examples of good current practice. Other aims were to stimulate teachers' interest in language teaching through dissemination of examples for local discussion, and to examine the material collected in the light of available theory. The evaluation of children's language use was informed by primary school teachers, and the material was collected in visits to, or as a result of visits to, many schools spread widely throughout the country. It is a reflection on our research values that the project should have been presented so diffidently by Connie Rosen as not calling for 'anything which could be dignified by the name of research'. But if we take a broader view of research than that of the experimental paradigm, and accept that a survey could be a very useful means of gleaning information, we do still have to ask how far this particular report paid off.

As research into language teaching the project was indirect. Observation of what children do – in the contexts in which they do it – necessarily includes and invites description of teaching practices. Although Connie Rosen was ostensibly looking for examples of language use she gleaned much information about teaching. It is clear that a present-day characteristic of primary schools is encouragement of children's talking, both with each other and with the teacher. One of the arts of teaching is the management of activity and of noise level to maximize desired conversation. It is also clear from the data collected that, in this situation, children from socio-economically disadvantaged backgrounds are not unwilling to talk, and can produce samples of language in use that are judged as very good. It is clear, too, that attention to language as such is not often shown, but that concentration by both teacher and pupil on the very varied activities of the day results in a considerable amount of very varied verbal exchange that is, in the course of events, naturally evaluated as to its appropriacy. One is reminded of the research that shows mothers attending more to the truth value of what their children say than to its precise grammatical form; and, most important, one sees the central issue as educational dialogue.

But while the sampling and reporting do give a reasonable basis for informing us about language teaching practices, how far can it tell us anything about their effectiveness? I am not asking that this should necessarily be described in terms of measured improvement on some test scale, but I am asking that, when samples of children's and teachers' talking are described as good, the criteria of judgement are spelled out, so that we know what kind of educational improvement we may look for when the term 'good' is applicable. Now I do not find much help with this question in the Rosen report. One may assume that an absence of talk would be said to be bad, but between this and the examples given there is nothing to indicate that one example is better than another. Instead, there is an attempt to select examples that are vaguely referred to as 'authentic' and as illustrating breadth of function. What is apparently valued is the varied use of language in description, question, explanation, reason and interpretation. Now I doubt whether anyone would dispute the importance of such variety, but is it the case that teaching is fostering it where it did not exist, or was less well-developed, before; or is the teaching simply allowing expression of which the children are already capable? It is not enough to say that teachers' language strategies can be internalized by the pupils, for we need to know whether they are in fact so internalized and, if so, how they are.

Nor can we confidently claim that children learn through the teachers' interpreting 'the children's meanings to themselves'. This raises the questions of the reliance that can be placed on the attribution of particular functions to speech acts, and of the relationship between use and learning. It is a lack of clarity in these matters that makes the Rosen research less useful than it might have been, but before I comment further on a 'functional' approach to language learning and assessment, I should like to draw attention to my last selected example of research.

This is a very different piece of work from the other research in that it is more a teacher-training project than a language teaching or learning investigation. I refer to Joan Tough's work in her Schools Council funded project 'Communication Skills in Early Childhood' (Tough 1976, 1977). It was originally based on an exploration of deficit or difference in disadvantaged children, that might be remedied by appropriate educational action. The original work has problems of sampling and method that have been discussed recently by G. Wells (1977); but I do not propose to pursue them here, because the research has since developed more as an attempt to foster a general and widely applicable approach to the development of the effective use of language. The essential feature is that the aspect of language to be developed is *meaning* or *function* – the two unfortunately not being clearly discriminated. This is to be achieved through the teacher's guidance, after careful appraisal of children's language use. In so far as Tough has organized and carried through an extensive programme of disseminating materials and ideas for discussion by country-wide groups of teachers, the work has been impressive; but I think that the project raises the same fundamental questions about attributing function to speech acts as are raised by the Rosen work, and these I shall treat as my fourth point in the following discussion.

Discussion of Review

1   *Evaluation procedures*

Now that features of the more significant recent early education language teaching research in this country have been reviewed, we can assess the question of the appropriacy of the evaluation procedures used. Obviously, in the intervention programmes, the classical experimental paradigm was widely adopted and ran into considerable difficulty. Now I do happen to think that, in certain contexts, the experimental approach is appropriate and useful; but it is clear that in educational contexts the control of both treatment and extraneous variables is virtually impossible, and even the basic requirement of random or controlled allocation of pupils to treatments can rarely be achieved. But there were, to my mind, even graver difficulties about its use in the language intervention programmes – not in the practical or ethical, but in the theoretical context.

The experimental paradigm is suited to either a systematic manipulation of a treatment in order to explore its effects on a *theoretically related* variable, or to comparing the effects of various treatments which would *theoretically predict* different kinds or degrees of change in a variable. In the intervention studies I do not think that the language variables were sufficiently well defined to be the bases of either the selection of treatments or the choice of measures of change. Nor do I think that the relationships of treatments or outcomes to the initial states of the children carried any sound theoretical weight. Only if the following questions could be clearly answered, would the experimental approach be appropriate. First – what is the defined nature of the deficit or difference to be remedied? Second – why should the selected treatment be expected to remedy the deficit or difference? Third – can suitable measures be found to relate to both the deficit or difference *and* the rationale of treatment? The reports of the various projects show the difficulties that were experienced with these questions.

If the experimental paradigm was inappropriate, what might have been a better approach? I think the answers to this come from the repeated comment that we needed to know what was actually happening. How did the children use language? How were the programmes implemented when it came to the actual teaching and learning? Were there any signs to the teachers that change was being effected in any way? How did the teachers fit the programmes into their teaching methods and philosophies? I am suggesting that what was needed was a much closer observational technique, with attention to the kind of feedback teachers and researchers were obtaining. Where this kind of data is reported we begin to find useful information for decisions about the nature and effectiveness of the interventions. In retrospect we can only wish there was more.

2 *The relation between language and other skills*

Arising in part from the question of the control of variables in an experimental procedure, but also arising directly from the review of projects, is the point that language teaching was much confused with more general nursery teaching. It is difficult to find clarity in aim in this matter. Indeed, the clearest picture comes from the Dundee project, which turned from a language orientation to a *concept attainment* aim. This was combined with a structured approach that predicted improvement in certain discrimination and conceptual skills in such a way that appropriate measures could be selected from language and intelligence tests. The choice of measures was rationally linked with the predicted change. The twin difficulties with the language development programmes were the lack of definition of aspects of spoken language ability to be improved, and the reluctance of teachers both to separate language education from an 'education of the whole child' approach, and to use 'training' methods in the context of a child-centred philosophy of teaching. Thus, although language, intellectual and social development can be neatly partitioned in theory, they were not so distinguished in the practical matter of teaching. It is not difficult to see how this came about in the absence of clear definition of language aims. When the general intervention instruction was effectively 'Use PLDK, adapting as you think necessary', then the outcome was likely to be a series of PLDK training sessions superimposed on the run of ordinary nursery days. The effect was likely to be a small, but specific shift in any test scores likely to be affected by the training (as the ITPA, for example), but no over-all change in the children's experience or use of language. The latter would largely reflect experience in the rest of their schooling and their life outside. When the general intervention instruction was effectively, 'Increase the amount children talk about their experience', the teachers' response was inevitably to be concerned with materials, techniques and groupings of children. *Experience of what?* became crucial, and this inevitably brought in problems of possibly restricting children's language if the experience was not novel, or of extending *at the same time* their social, intellectual and language growth if it was new. Thus if children talked more it might only be that they were doing what they could always have done if invited by the teacher, and if the forms or uses of their speech changed in any way then it still might be that they could have done so before if the 'right' experiences had been used. Did the experience actually influence their language development; or did it influence their perceptions and thinking, and so indicate better what might be talked about? In retrospect, we can see that we have not the kind of data to begin to answer these questions.

That practical difficulties should arise in clarifying the relationship of language to other forms of learning is perhaps not surprising when we look at the state of theory on this question. I doubt whether, on theoretical grounds, we can say anything very much about likely effects of language training on language or cognitive development, nor of the effects of other learning on language development. We should need to be able to say, on theoretical grounds, that a particular experience is necessary for a particular development. I think it possible that certain language 'input' conditions and certain experiences of cognitive change might qualify, but I see no signs behind the intervention programmes of the kind of rigorous analysis of language and cognitive development that any such decision would entail.

3   *The nature of deficit or difference*

My third discussion point relates to the question of the theoretical relationship between treatment and effect on the target population. Here one question is the nature of the change to be aimed for, not as a simple matter of language development as in any young school child, but as a matter of especial relevance for the disadvantaged. The other is the basis for expecting that a selected treatment would achieve the desired change. Now it seems to me that none of the intervention programmes were clear on these matters. The questions were possibly not even seen as problematic by the Gahagans, for they seemed to feel that all that was needed was the right kind of standardized test to measure the aspects of language then thought to distinguish the restricted and elaborated codes as sketched out by Bernstein. The then current view was that differences in some linguistic codes as they affected education might be ironed out by compensatory treatment. What the disadvantaged needed for schooling, but lacked by virtue of the difference, could be made up. The difficulty with this theoretical viewpoint is that the nature of the relevant difference has never been shown. Differences in the use of language in different social contexts have been suggested by various researchers, but it has become increasingly clear that the disadvantaged can often 'pull out' all the uses shown by middle-class children of the same age, though not necessarily as frequently, or over the same range of contexts. (This is, of course, not true for immigrant children for whom English is a second and only very partially learned language. I think their case would be best dealt with in an entirely different discussion, and shall, therefore, leave it aside.) Nevertheless, while we have found it increasingly difficult to pin down a Bernstein-type difference that has been shown to be both real and educationally relevant, most of the intervention research has continued to show the pattern of less well developed school-relevant vocabulary and concept attainment, and of lag in development of more complex forms of spoken English, that we have known for a long time to be common in the educationally less successful and in lower-working-class children. It seems to me, therefore, that in the absence of an empirically supported theory of language difference, the only firm case we have for intervening in the language development of the disadvantaged child must rest on this kind of deficit and retardation. We could try to extend vocabulary and to improve command of structural complexity in verbal expression *as they are required in accordance with educational practice in schools*. This is not to say that we may not wish to achieve other ends, such as increased willingness to talk in educational contexts, but these ends would relate to the context of learning, not to what is to be learned.

4   *The problem of defining language measures in terms of function*

The three points I should like to raise are the validity and reliability of attributing functions to speech acts, the relationship between language use and language learning, and the bearing of language function on learning in general.

On the first point, I do not find in Rosen, in Tough, nor even in Halliday (1975) on whose work the others lean heavily, any very clear indication about how one goes about attributing function to remarks. What it seems to me to entail is inference on the part of the observer or listener – inference based on evidence as to the speaker's intended effect or effects, and inference based on the linguistic conventions he adopts. Thus inferred intentions must be based on both regular behavioural evidence and regular linguistic form, and the grounds for inference can, in principle, be spelled out. What I find in fact is a very sketchy approach in Halliday, and just about no evidence for inference in Rosen and in Tough. There is a jump from the description of utterances to an attribution of function of some kind; and I must confess that I do not share their confidence that, as a hearer, I know enough about a child's general behaviour patterns in various contexts, nor about his linguistic conventions, to take his meaning and intention without error. I should have to know the child very well indeed to be so confident, and I therefore question how much agreement between myself and others could be reasonably obtained in attributing functions and meanings to young children's speech when the children are not very well known by us. I am, therefore, doubting the validity and reliability of the 'functional' descriptions of child speech that are to be found in the literature. They may be adequate, but we are given insufficient evidence for confidence.

On the second point, I should like to see language development defined as the developing command of conventional forms of expression within the speech community of a child's upbringing, and of the grasp of the range and occasions of appropriate expressions. (This use of the term 'conventional' is simply to convey that language structure is regular, and socially agreed, and the basis of mutual comprehension – it is not intended to imply lack of creative opportunity.) With this view of the development of linguistic behaviour the meanings signified and symbolized in a speech act could not be divorced from the actual vocabulary and syntax adopted. To talk of function is not to move away from these latter, but to make their importance more clear, for to develop the expression of meaning is to command more and more effectively the available forms of language. Language use in itself might even be static, in the sense that a child might simply be doing what he has been able to do for some time, but learning further uses would be the means to further structural knowledge. Equally, attention drawn to a new structure might open up a new range of function.

Now it seems to me that the functions described by Halliday and by Tough are at a rather vague level of generality, so that they are in principle attributable in some measure to the speech of very young children indeed, and they do not discriminate, except possibly in relative frequency of use, between children of different ages or social backgrounds. Tough in fact concedes the latter, but does not attend to the former. A point I wish to emphasize most strongly is that the difference between the kind of dialogue between 3½-year-old children reported by Tough (1976, p. 77) and that I have observed with a 2½-year-old is not a difference of range of function as described in Tough's terms, but of command of syntax and vocabulary. I suspect that due regard to these differences might allow a much finer analysis of the probable intentions and meanings expressed in children's speech, and a better account of language development. Such an endeavour might also provide a more useful framework for the study of educational dialogue, and for recommendations about both language and more general teaching.

On the third point, I understand the tenor of the Rosens' and of Tough's work to be that language use facilitates general learning. This I find to be a possibility rather than a general truth. The burden of the language intervention programmes has been that increased attention to language is not in itself very productive, but that 'good nursery practice' which entails the sharing of new experiences by teacher and child within 'cognitively' and 'socially' orientated schooling facilitates both language *and* more general learning. The two march hand in hand. To talk to some purpose is simply to be human, to talk to some educational purpose is to promote teaching and learning. In devoting attention to the functions of language we need not only to spell out the criteria by which we infer intentions and meanings but also to discriminate those features of dialogue that promote learning.

My conclusions, made with benefit of hindsight, must be that much of the research reviewed here has been a story of struggling for some insight into the nature of language learning and teaching as it takes place in schools, rather than a series of interventions that could clearly show the effects of various kinds of teaching. The premise of social-class-based deficit or difference, on which much of the research rested, was not firmly based; improvement in those features of language that had traditionally been assessed was not reckoned to be the crucial issue in much of the intervention, and there was no spelling out of other criteria; the whole place of language teaching in the early school curriculum was not at all clear. The important question now arising is the kind of effect this rather confused and confusing effort has had on teachers.

Effects of Research on Teachers

These effects can be viewed in several ways. I shall choose to examine both the reported effects of the reviewed projects and the effects of the research on the practice of nursery and primary school teaching more generally.

Effects on the project teachers

An obvious question to ask is the nature of reactions to the whole idea of a special language teaching intervention. There was clearly a marked reluctance on the part of many teachers to separate language learning from other learning in early education. This was intensified by the nature of the Peabody approach, which was seen as emphasizing separation by its 'twenty-minute session' nature, by its content, and by the implication that special training over and above that of experienced nursery teachers was needed for language teaching. Woodhead reported that teachers felt that their own training made such a programme unnecessary, but that nursery assistants, who were closer to the untrained personnel for whom the PLDK was designed, reacted more favourably. Quigley (1971) made a similar observation of reactions in the EPA projects. But even where the PLDK was not used, or was adapted to the teacher's views, there were still grave doubts about the separation of language training from the language experience of everyday exchange in the nursery school. It was interesting that adaptations and developments moved in the direction of closer integration with other aims and activities, of one-to-one interaction with the child, and of conversation, rather than other structured exercises in aspects of language development.

Linked with reactions to the idea of a separate approach was the problem of seeing a programme as an entity, rather than as a collection of possible teaching/learning tasks and materials. Barnes, Woodhead, Halsey and Quigley reported a tendency for teachers to concentrate on the minutiae of programmes rather than on an over-all policy, and this was to be found in both hostile and receptive teachers. Woodhead noticed criticism of individual lessons or materials in the PLDK without reference to their place in the programme as a whole. Barnes reported that structured conversation pieces became ends in themselves rather than being supplements to a spoken language curriculum. One reason for this kind of reaction may have lain in bewilderment as to the aims of the programmes. Barnes, reporting on the Deptford Junior School work, remarked that language work seemed a solution without a rational justification, and many of the teachers were not clear as to why they were implementing it. Another reason may have lain in the expectation of language improvement without any clear idea about assessing or defining it, so that the work itself became its own justification. A third reason may have been related to teachers' normal planning time-spans. Do they plan for each day, day by day; or do they engage in long-term planning, relating a whole series of days' work in structured ways? And a fourth reason may be that the exercise of finding tasks and materials, or imaginatively inventing activities, is so demanding that it takes up the teachers' attention, and there is nothing left for consideration of what the activity is all in aid of. If the last two reasons are valid, then the language programmes were not introducing new kinds of reaction, but simply bringing to the surface those already there in normal teaching.

Other reactions to the projects revealed different interpretations of language teaching. These variously referred to dealing with concept-formation, dialect problems, grammatical construction and error, vocabulary, spelling, fluency, communication, comprehension and reading. Barnes reported teachers' resistance to theoretical analyses of language, whether socio-linguistic, syntactic, phonetic or functional – they preferred to speak in everyday terminology at an everyday level. This fragmentary approach fitted better into attending to aspects of language within ordinary teaching, than into either a cohesive programme or a developmental outlook.

Effects on the teachers personally were varied, and tended to relate in part to their initial attitude to a programme. Those who were hostile but who were involved in trying out a programme seemed relatively impervious (Quigley 1971), and attributed any improvement in children's language to their non-programme experience. They seemed sure of their own abilities and the effectiveness of their usual teaching. Those who were more receptive tended to report an increase in awareness of what was going on in their class-rooms and especially in awareness of children's activities and knowledge. Quigley reported some as being 'appalled to realize what children didn't know'. Some gained in confidence in their own abilities in curriculum development, and some developed a more structured approach in their own teaching. A few remained worried by the conflict between their philosophy of nursery education with its emphasis on learning through discovery, and children's evident enjoyment of a structured and even 'drilled' experience. But perhaps what disturbed teachers most was the raising of the question of evaluation of teaching methods and approaches. In particular, Barnes and Quigley reported them as disliking the experience of finding that an emotional or damning reaction on their part was not a sufficient basis for making a judgement of a programme. Further reasons had to be sought.

A final effect of intervention programmes worth mentioning is that of influencing the teachers' perceptions of children. The chief danger is that of introducing and hardening stereotypes. The association of social background with possible language deficit or difference has tended to define 'the Bernstein child' as lower-working-class, able to talk only a little and in brief, ungrammatical forms, unable to make use of a variety of language functions, and resistant to education. Woodhead's discussion of teachers' reactions tends to make this point, and it seems to me that the encouragement of stereotyping is a real danger in Tough's work. Teachers may begin to see children as the theory describes them, rather than as they really are.

I shall now turn to the question of the effects of research on teachers who were not involved in the various projects. To this end, I shall report on a small survey I recently made in a northern city.

Effects of language teaching research on practising teachers

The questionnaire was designed to give information about sources of ideas, present views and practice and any recent changes in provision of language teaching. It gave anonymity to responding teachers, but yielded detail about catchment area and type of school. It was circulated with the help of the local education authority to head teachers of 100 primary schools in the area, and replies were received from thirty-three. Their distribution according to various characteristics is shown in Table 2.1.

Table 2.1   Percentages in each category of schools in the sample

Location	%	Social background	%	Age range	%
				years	
Inner city	12	Lower working class	21	3–5	6
Inner suburban	25	Mixed working class	36	3–7	6
Outer suburban	50	Mixed working and middle class	30	3–9	24
Rural and semi-rural	12	Mostly middle class	12	3–12	9
				5–7	12
				5–9	30
				5–12	12

While representative sampling cannot possibly be claimed, a useful spread was achieved nevertheless. A further important characteristic of schools in the area was the proportion of children of immigrant origin whose native tongue was not English. In six of the schools (18 per cent), English was not the native tongue of the home for more than 5 per cent of the children. In one school the figure was 70 per cent. Five of the six were inner-city schools in a lower-working-class catchment area, but the other was in an outer suburban industrial area with a mixed social class background. A further eight schools made provision for some kind of special language teaching for such children of immigrant origin, but all fourteen gave information that also showed attention to language teaching for non-immigrants. The other nineteen schools claimed to have no children of non-English speaking origin.

Replies to a question asking for views about special language teaching for various categories of children showed that all but four schools felt it to be essential for *all children*, though the question did not allow any distinction between special separate language teaching and special emphasis within the normal curriculum. Reasons given were sometimes tautological but included reference to improving vocabulary, grammar, fluency, use, expression of thought and reasoning, reading and writing. Why special emphasis was thought to be needed was not at all clear. For lower-working-class children, however, concepts of deficiency were to be found in the reasons given. Only one reply indicated that not all such children 'articulated poorly'. Of the other thirty-two, five abstained from responding, four gave no reason for saying that special help was needed, seven gave similar reasons to those for all children, seven gave reasons of deficiencies in the children's language or speech, while *nine gave reasons of deficiencies in the home without reference to the child's abilities.* A further point was that many of the replies indicated strong pressure on children who did not show much inclination to talk. More talking was a valued, but largely unjustified, aim; but one reply suggested that conversation could have diagnostic usefulness, and another suggested caution in face of shyness and possible special problems.

Responses to questions about practice within the schools were much lower than those to the factual questions about the type of school, the catchment area and provision for different categories of pupils. To a question asking for up to six reports, books or materials relating to language development that had been discussed among the staff, 30 per cent supplied no information. The others, however, provided a wide range of suggestions covering various aspects of spoken and written language skills. For the most part these were kits, materials and guide books supplied by educational publishers; a few were more general books on language teaching or learning. Access to research seemed to be principally through the Bullock Report (thirteen mentions) and Tough's Schools Council publications. The latter had sometimes been introduced by a teacher who had attended a course in the Schools Council project or had found them available at the local teachers' centre.

A question asking which such reports, books or materials had been found useful tended to elicit the same range of suggestions. The reasons given for their usefulness suggested an insatiable need for materials of all kinds that would be used to focus conversation with pupils and between pupils. Audio-visual aids, including BBC programmes, were frequently appreciated. When reasons over and above encouragement of conversation were given, they suggested value in pinpointing the learning of specific skills in listening and in phonic approaches to reading.

When questioned about shortcomings in any language programme that had been used, only four schools responded, choosing to mention as programmes *Language in Action*, *Listening to Children Talking* (Tough), and *SRA Reading Workshop*. The criticisms included being helpful but not being a solution to the language teaching problem, dangers of a record-centred rather than child-centred approach, and insufficient material of various kinds. It seemed that, while the teachers were very busily engaged in seeking materials and guidance and were making the best use of whatever they had, criticism may have seemed to them a luxury they could not afford or attend to, rather than an essential attitude to new provision.

When asked what further help they would like, if any, in their language teaching, the chief needs expressed were for more teachers and more resources, in that order. Two replies appreciated speech therapist help and asked for more, and only one reply asked for more information about aims behind programmes. The response rate was surprisingly low for the question. Perhaps the teachers felt overwhelmed already (as some replies suggested), or perhaps they felt they were managing very well as they were.

On the assumption that it was possible that respondents might feel that too much stress had been placed on language teaching, they were given a chance to agree or disagree and give reasons. Again there was a reluctance to make a judgement, only a third actually responding. This was perhaps the question most likely to expose uncertainty as to the aims and importance of language teaching. Of those who did respond, most emphasized its importance, and even asked for more stress on language teaching; but most simply gave tautological reasons. Only three replies qualified its importance. One felt that, in some schools at least, language teaching need not be seen as a special feature, but would be best interpreted in the whole approach; another stressed the danger of destroying enjoyment through over-emphasis, while a third felt it was being stressed 'beyond the point of realism' and into minute detail.

A final question asked whether practice in language teaching had been changed in any way in the last two years, and teachers were invited to indicate the nature of any change. Here only four failed to respond, but twelve indicated no change, while seventeen indicated change and some spelled out its nature. Only one of those with no change went so far as to say it was not considered necessary – that staffing, equipment and methods were together able to meet the problem. The direction was towards more attention, time, staffing and resources being devoted to language teaching, both in special separate school activities and in the ordinary run of class-room activities. The nature of the shift in teaching was often towards more small group or individual-based conversation, with attention being paid to the ways children spoke; but mention was made of more structured programmes, special language rooms, and more use of audio-visual aids. It was also the case that attention to spoken language went hand-in-hand with that to reading, and that the encouragement of listening and discrimination skills was emphasized.

The final point of interest in the responses was a clear correlation between report of change and the presence of a nursery unit in the school. The distribution is shown in Table 2.2:

Table 2.2

Age range (years)	Type of school			
	With nursery		Without nursery	
	Change	No change	Change	No change
3 to 5	2	0		
3 or 5 to 7	1	1	0	4
3 or 5 to 9	7	1	4	6
3 or 5 to 12	2	1	1	3
Total	12	3	5	13

There was no relationship between catchment social background and change, but a slight tendency for more change to be reported in inner suburban schools. Whether the change took place entirely at the nursery level, or whether nursery teaching influenced teaching in the rest of the school, could not be determined.

When I pull together the interpretations of replies to the questionnaire the main findings seem to be:

i.   a recent strengthening of interest in language teaching, especially with the younger children and with reading;

ii.   more attention to educational publishers' materials than to research publications;

iii.   a concentration of attention on staffing, organization of pupils, and resources for teaching purposes;

iv.   a lack of attention to aims and effectiveness;

v.   a very vague and global understanding of the role of language in learning;

vi.   attention to aspects of language skill such as fluency, articulation, vocabulary, grammatical error and reading ability rather than to language development.

vii.   some stereotyping of children according to perceived home background;

viii.   an assertion of teacher competence in the face of perceived inadequacies in pupils;

ix.   a sense in teachers of being pressured and sometimes overwhelmed in the area of language teaching.

These findings are similar to those of the language teaching research projects, and show that the impact of research on the teachers has not been a direct taking up of ideas and approaches, but an increase in attention to familiar aspects of language and to materials supplied by educational publishers. These may or may not be aware of research trends, and will in any case interpret perceived needs in their own way.

How do we stand now for the future?

The research thrust would seem to be along three related lines – clarification of patterns and processes of language development, the effect of differences in language abilities on attainment in school, and what actually happens in the class-room in the course of teaching and learning. The emphasis in this last is on teacher accountability, rather than outcome testings of pupils. Teachers may welcome the first two directions of research, though only if reports are couched in terms they find comprehensible; but are they likely to approve the last? This is a crucial question when the whole matter of assessment of performance is being raised generally by the DES. Whose performance should be assessed? Who is accountable to whom and for what? These questions cut at the heart of the problems of teaching, requiring a close look at values, aims and effectiveness as well as at actual practice. Can such a look help teachers to a heightened sense of professional responsibility so that they ask these questions of themselves, and can be given opportunities to explore them in both initial and in-service training? Or will it lead, as seems possible from some of the reactions to research so far, to a closing of the ranks through fear of possible exposure and loss of freedom? Much may depend on the way research is conducted.

This paper was presented to the SCRE Seminar in Stirling in July 1978.

3

Between the Mother's Dialect and English

The role of the standard language of the country of origin in a community of southern Italian immigrants and its position in the linguistic education of their children.[1]

ARTURO TOSI

Introduction

In recent years hectic consultations have taken place in Europe, and particularly in Britain, on the question of teaching children of immigrants in school the language spoken at home. The debate, which has spread rapidly to circles of teachers, academics, administrators and people active in minority community organizations, is clearly related to the wider, and more complex questions of the position, rights and future of a minority population in a multi-ethnic society. Among those involved in this debate it now seems possible to identify at least three definite and different positions.[2]

Some seem to believe that the presence of a variety of ethnic groups in a society is a good enough reason to define that society as multicultural, as if multi-ethnicism automatically meant multiculturalism. The argument is that everyone is free to retain his own traditions, habits and culture, while the responsibility for establishing policies and measures for their maintenance concerns the minority community organizations alone. Many others support the view that Britain's educational system is still too solidly based on monocultural premises and penalizes minority groups' children. They contend that, if a country claims to take into account the diversity of its population, this should be reflected in a school curriculum that recognizes and promotes cultural pluralism. Finally others – who share with the previous group this view that diversity should be reproduced by the curriculum of the mainstream school – disagree deeply with everyone else on the design of the linguistic policy to be introduced into a multi-ethnic school. They maintain that a multicultural and monolingual curriculum is a useless palliative in a society that claims to promote cultural pluralism. In fact they point out that historical evidence and research show that multi-cultural interaction cannot survive without the media that embody the different cultures, and that multiculturalism cannot be genuinely achieved without an adequate policy of multilingualism. However, teachers and educationists in Educational Priority Areas feel they cannot wait for the conclusion of the debate in which political declarations of intent contend with everyday reality, policies of 'genuine multi-culturalism' with separative cultural diversity and bilingualism with semilingualism.[3] They point out that there are serious problems to be faced with minority children and that these problems concern, above all, language: for the children habitually speak at home a language different from that taught in the school.

Mother Tongue, Dialect and Standard Language

The few pilot schemes that have been set up by LEAs are now looked to with extreme interest by both researchers and practitioners for their potential in setting out new trends, emphasizing old ones or, indeed, in establishing future policies.[4] Suddenly a strong interest seems to have developed in 'the other language' of the minority child and, although there might not be agreement on the position and the future of those 'other languages' in this society, certainly it seems to be agreed that they deserve some recognition in schools. The same position is also held by some international organizations such as the Council of Europe and the European Parliament. These, following UNESCO's example, have reiterated recommendations to member governments that special linguistic provision should be made for children who are 'non nationals', bringing into the class-room a language different from that in which teaching is done in the school. In particular the Council of Ministers of the European Community approved in July 1977 a Directive (which will come into force in 1981) according to which 'member states should take appropriate measures to promote the teaching of the mother tongue and of the culture of the country of origin' to children who are non nationals.[5] The atmosphere seems favourable for spreading concern and sensitizing educationists and administrators to undertake positive action and set up new programmes. However, the differing social situations in which linguistic problems develop in various ethnic minority groups must be considered if schemes are to be successfully planned and future disappointments stemming from over-eager ill-informed enthusiasm avoided.

Indeed it would appear a necessary and preliminary operation for the educationist concerned with the 'mother tongue' problem to make in his investigation specific reference to the different languages spoken in the communities, e.g. Punjabi, Italian, Bengali, Portuguese, etc. The term 'mother tongue', if used without reference to an ethnic group, is now in serious danger of eliciting misinformed discussion and misleading conclusions. Thus one of the first tasks of the educationist is to define the different positions of those ethnic languages present in the community. The roles of such languages in the home, their uses in the community, the degrees of distance between the dialects spoken and the standard varieties taught, and the level of social usefulness of the two varieties, all differ at home; there are also in Britain differences in the values and traditions that they embody, the sympathy and acceptance of their associated cultures by new generations, the social and psychological motives for learning them, and the professional view of them resulting from their differing status as 'immigrants' languages' or 'languages of culture' for the indigenous, educated middle class. All these cannot be dealt with by the educationist if he uses 'mother tongue' as a blanket term to cover any language that is not English.

Also important is the ambiguity inherent in the term 'mother tongue' within the context of the specific community where a minority language is spoken. 'Mother tongue' means one's native tongue: in the case of minority children it is their first language, the 'other idiom' that they bring to school and that they have learnt from their parents. But to what extent does this language correspond to the 'mother tongue of the country of origin' which, in the terminology of the EEC Directive and indeed in the practical teaching situation, is the national standard language of their country of origin? If we analyse this problem in the context of a particular minority group, and in relation to the specific socio-linguistic conditions of its members, we will discover that the two aims of (1) maintaining and developing the child's home language in the school, and (2) teaching the 'mother tongue and culture of the country of origin' do not necessarily coincide in all minority groups.

First of all, one must bear in mind that the vast majority of the foreign population to whom we refer when we talk about language diversity in Britain are immigrant workers. And one must also acknowledge that those who had to leave their own country were precisely those who suffered most from lack of educational provision at home. This has resulted in their alienation from the qualifying values of the national/dominant culture and, so, in their inability to compete socially. Furthermore we must also acknowledge the fact that, over and above the effects of class and culture, immigrants such as the Italians, with whom we are concerned in this paper, often belong to a minority group even at home (Sardinians, Ladins, Friulians, and also Sicilians, Calabrians and Campani) and are speakers of minority languages with no recognized status. Naturally, this has been one of the principal factors in distancing the cultural reality of their past from privileged cultural expressions standardized by developing national trends of urban and industrial culture, which are the only ones formalized in mainstream education constituting the syllabi of Italian language and culture teaching at home and abroad. However, limiting our considerations here to the question of language diversity, the notions of standard Italian and dialects need to be clarified.

As A. L. and G. Lepschy have recently pointed out,

> When people talk of Italian dialects they are not usually referring to different varieties of Italian. Italian dialects differ from literary Italian and among themselves so much that one dialect may be unintelligible to the speaker of another dialect. They may differ among themselves as much as French differs from Spanish, or Portuguese from Roumanian or, for that matter Italian from English. The initial effect of strangeness, foreignness and unintelligibility can be the same. The situation is of course different, because with Italian dialects, which derive from Latin and have had some cultural contact with literary Italian as it developed through the centuries, the establishment of a basis for mutual understanding, the identification of correspondence rules and the beginning of a translation and of a learning process are obviously so much easier. It has recently been suggested that, for some parts of Italy at least, one needs to distinguish between four strata[6]: besides (a) the national language and (b) the local dialect there is (c) a more inward looking variety of the national language (regional Italian), and (d) a more outward looking variety of the local dialect (regional dialect). Take a simple sentence like 'Go home, boys' as uttered in a village in Venetia. The allegedly standard form in the national language would be *andáte a kkása ragáttsi* and in the local dialect something like *ve káza túzi*. But in the same village people may also use a less local, more regional Venetian form like *nde káza tózi*, and a less national, more regional Italian form like *andáte a káza ragási* (Lepschy and Lepschy 1977).

Naturally the distinction between the four strata does not apply to language use in an Italian community abroad. In Britain, for instance, the situation is obviously complicated by the role played by English. However, the distinction matters to us in so far as it shows the distance between the language spoken at home by the first generation (local dialect) and the national standard language, which is the language to be taught in the classroom. Furthermore, we cannot ignore the fact that, in most communities of Italians abroad, and certainly in Britain, standard Italian is never used either in its written or spoken forms:

indeed it is not a language to which the second generation is ever exposed in the community. Describing the Italian socio-linguistic context Lepschy and Lepschy explain that, although Italian dialects may be unintelligible to the speaker of another dialect and/or standard Italian, the dialect speaker living in Italy is able to develop, to some extent, 'natural' means of transfer from dialect to standard Italian and vice versa. This process is reinforced by formal education in school, but is also certainly helped to a significant extent by exposure to standard Italian in the community where the national language is becoming more commonly used for both private and social functions.

But what is the degree of intelligibility of the standard language for dialect speakers, children of immigrants, born and brought up in a community abroad who, through total lack of exposure, cannot develop this 'natural' ability? In this new context it would seem that the access to communication is determined solely by the intrinsic structural similarities between the two media, both deriving from Latin. One could tentatively suggest that there must be forms and structures of standard Italian that the dialect speaker should be able to decode and, perhaps, reproduce with native ability, others that he should be able to decode with near-native ability, resulting in functional intelligibility despite the limited degree of accuracy and, finally, others to which he would feel, both in speaking and listening, totally foreign.

It could be claimed that it would not be impossible to design special strategies and teaching materials to guide in the class-room a process of transfer from dialect to standard Italian. To some extent, of course, this could create the conditions for helping children identify basic correspondence rules between the two languages.[7] In this paper, however, I do not intend to deal with defining the special learning conditions for Italian dialect-speaking children learning standard Italian abroad,[8] nor will I attempt to identify what is needed in the class-room to initiate and guide a transfer. This would involve extensive work of contrastive analysis of the structures of the two languages (a research project that would be of tremendous use to the linguistic and academic achievement of these children and which I hope will find the interest and financial support of some institution). The aim of this paper is to identify the role played by three languages (Italian dialect, standard Italian and English) in a community of workers from south Italy. This investigation developed from the need to clarify the status, position and use, among first and second generations, of three linguistic media, components of the multilingualism of a community of immigrants: an analysis that many are beginning to regard as a necessary preliminary to the effective introduction of provision for

minority language maintenance in a society that is considering accepting
and promoting bilingualism among its multi-ethnic population.[9]

The Italian Community in Bedford

Italian immigration[10]

Historically speaking Bedford is an English town. Today at first sight
Bedford is still a typical English town of the south Midlands: a population of 80,000, several hundred commuters to London, and a quiet river
flowing placidly under arched bridges – close to the picturesque market
square and the busy High Street. But behind the High Street and the
river banks one realizes that the traditional English Bedford is dead –
30 per cent of its people are now foreign immigrants – for more than
fifty nationalities are represented: ethnically Bedford is the most varied
town of its size in the United Kingdom. Since 1951, throughout the
1950s and into the 1960s southern Italians flooded into Bedford,
followed in more recent years by West Indians and Asians. Today
Italians are still probably the largest group, some 9000 – over 10 per
cent of the population. This makes Bedford the largest Italian settlement in the United Kingdom outside London, where the Italian
community is older, made up of more socially heterogeneous groups,
and much more scattered.[11] After the war, at a time when the United
States was closed to Italian immigration, when the luckiest southern
Italian labourer could emigrate only with a temporary contract to
Switzerland, France or Germany, the United Kingdom appeared to
Italian villagers not too far away to seek their fortune. In those years
the United Kingdom was facing the great postwar building boom and
the management of the London Brick Company – where the bulk of
British bricks are made – sent a mission to Naples to recruit labour.
The 'bulk recruitment scheme' was launched, as the papers commented,
to solve the desperate shortage of English labourers, most of them
unwilling to do the tough, dirty work in the brickfields. The company
management were more than satisfied with their programme: 'without
the Italians, we don't know what we should do' a company official said
and the scheme in fact succeeded in luring some thousands of
unemployed Italians who were taken on at the Bedford brickyards with
four-year contracts. Their families and children were left at home, in
the villages in Sicily or Campania. The 'flood' of southern Italian
labourers in Bedford continued thoughout the 1950s and soon two-
thirds of the Brick Company's labour force were Italian.

The young Italians lived in hostels working hard and saving money so as to remit a large portion of their wages to their families in Italy. 'They are prepared to work all hours – they don't suffer from tea-breakitis, they positively thrive on overtime – even two full eight hours shifts a day' a company official commented.[12] After some years spent between the hostel and the one-roomed accommodation in large Victorian houses, where workers on different shifts often shared the same bed, many Italians obtained a certificate of satisfactory conduct from their employer. This document, together with a landlord's notification of willingness to accommodate Italian people in his lodging, eventually opened Bedford's doors to the labourer's family: the migrant worker had become an official resident immigrant and the Italian community in Bedford was formed. Of the 9000 southern Italians living in Bedford (several more thousands live in neighbouring industrial areas, Nottingham, Peterborough, St Albans, Cambridge, etc.) more than half came from just three rather remote villages: Busso in Molise, Montefalcione in Campania and S. Angelo Muxaro in Sicily – although there are also some representatives from Calabria, Basilicata and Puglia.

The process is known as 'chain immigration', a mechanism of expatriation that has always proved to southern Italians an efficient way of finding a good reception and help abroad. When the individual village develops links with a particular destination, strong family and kinship ties make those who are well established abroad more clearly obliged to help their co-villagers to join them. This was in fact the case with Italian immigrants to the United States and Australia, but in the Bedford adventure, the chain immigration did not produce the same effect. The family and kinship did not compensate for the risk of the expedition since their compatriots could not offer more than some information on new vacancies at the London Brick Company or vague promises of an introduction to a landlord. Unlike other cases of departure for a common destination – following the pattern of a chain immigration process, where members of the community abroad attract other families and they themselves act as leaders reorganizing the community abroad – individual Italians in Bedford had no role to play in organizing their community. Men were the first to be taken in, women and children followed, after them old people. Over a period of eight years the original community was dismantled, reassembled and encapsulated in Bedford.[13]

The development of this movement had remarkable consequences both in the establishment of the community abroad, and in the attitude of the people towards their native village and home country. The men's total ignorance of their future and that of their families, people's frustration at seeing the original village being deprived first of its able-bodied men, then of its families and eventually of most institutions, must have suggested that the village was gradually going to die. To southern Italian villagers, strongly attached to their community and respectful of its values, the prospect of a possible disappearance of their home in Italy must have seemed like the loss of their whole background and identity, so closely related to their visual memorization of the village, its features and life. This fear, which reinforced the individual's tendency to retain his original customs and values in the new foreign environment, was just as strong as the feelings of security and protection he derived from sharing the neighbourhood with co-villagers in a street in Bedford. This phenomenon of extreme conservatism appears to be further reinforced by the special terms of their employment, for so many years a short-term renewable contract. The labourers, recruited for a limited period of time, arrived feeling that, however long their residence might be, their stay could be ended at any time. A return to Italy would be facilitated by their savings which would be adequate to open some business in a southern Italian village or town.

In these conditions it would seem that Italian people in Bedford, constantly fostering the dream of returning home, had faced and accepted their new environment as outsiders, like the seasonal migrant workers in Switzerland or Germany. Certainly the majority never really showed – or show – the disposition and determination of an immigrant, who has taken the step of becoming a permanent settler in a foreign land. In addition to this we must consider the fear of losing contact with their village – not out of choice, but because they were unwittingly caught up in a process of alienation from the original background. In fact we shall see that these two factors have affected enormously the process of protection of self-image against the acceptance of the new country's culture, habits and values.

Social conditions of Italians

In Bedford the Italian man's social life is restricted to the circles of his compatriots: introduction and friendships are made exclusively through the contacts of the family and the extended family. In his free time an Italian man is never seen on his own; but when he is not at home with his family, only other men of his own family, kinship group or 'compari'[14] come into his social life. Also Italian men do not indulge much in activities such as sports and games, nor do they seem to have many individual friends.

While the principal limiting factor in the men's social life is long working hours, virtually none of the women has any real social life at all. Unlike in the Italian village, almost all Italian women living in Bedford have a job. Their routine is an exhausting one: often two shifts separated by a lunch break, during which they do their housework and the cooking for the family, who will gather in the evening. Women's social contacts develop especially with other Italian women working in the same establishment: hospitals, factories or cleaning offices and public buildings. Women are in charge of the shopping and maintenance of the house which, beside work, offer the two other main occasions for their social interaction in the neighbourhood.

Social life, in the sense of either public activities or small group gatherings, does not seem to take place within the Italian community, possibly because all energies are spent at work and all resources used to improve living conditions and to increase savings. Apart from a few men's clubs, where the men occasionally play cards and other games, there are no public places where Italian people and families can meet. However, regular inter-community family contacts do not seem to have developed much further since the time of departure, as it is known that family ties are still very largely those that were originated in the village at home. The only opportunities for large social gatherings are offered by a wedding, when the family group meets with its extended network of relations and 'compari' and with acquaintances. A marriage for Italian people in Bedford is still an occasion for showing to the whole community the family's concern for their children, their consent to the child's choice and the family's prosperity.

In such circumstances, and in the light of their causes tentatively outlined in the previous section, it is understandable that the first generation's contacts with the world outside their community, and particularly the English group, should be extremely limited in frequency and intensity. Attachment to original customs, faith in ancestral social values and appreciation of different individual qualities – reinforced by apprehension at losing them in a foreign environment – have progressively centred the aspirations of Italian people in Bedford within the boundaries of their own community. Outside the community, the English group appears to Italian eyes too distant, too ethnocentric and unwilling to mix. English Bedfordians do not seem to hide their resentment of the various ethnic groups settling in their town, and they certainly disapproved of the Italian settlement.

At the level of individual interrelationships between the two groups there is an insignificant number of mixed marriages, even among the second generation, as against the in-group marriages of young people who met in Bedford or who were 'introduced' by the parents during holidays in Italy. At the level of inter-group social compatibility and integration, the postwar urban development in Bedford reveals some significant facts. It appears that the centre of the town, with its old Victorian houses situated close to the river bank – pride of the nostalgic Bedfordians – has not yet benefited from the new restoration plan for the town's development which is developing modern suburban areas more in keeping with what the natives want.

Consequently in Bedford today the deliberate introvert tendency among the Italian minority, not significantly tempered by the effect of the local environment, has led to marked isolation of first generation Italians. This has resulted in an extreme preservation of original traits and in lack of appreciation of habits and culture outside their community. Naturally this isolation – originally created in Italy by socially and culturally disadvantaged conditions, and further reinforced by the impact of an alien environment – could not fail to have strong repercussions at a communicative level. We shall see, in fact, that they have produced a parallel form of linguistic isolation characterized by phenomena of semibilingualism without diglossia. These phenomena closely involve psychological conflicts in the second generation where they are liable to produce effects in language development that result in serious educational and social disadvantages.

Multilingualism in the Italian Community

Multilingualism in the first generation

Three main varieties of Italian dialect are spoken in Bedford: 'Molisano', 'Campano-Irpino' and a South-Western variety of Sicilian.[15] For most first generation Italians, one of those dialects is the mother tongue learnt and developed in the village in Italy. For a small minority the dialect learnt in the village in Italy was further developed in Bedford. This is the case with first generation Italians who arrived in Bedford as children or adolescents and who naturally present linguistic and cultural features of neither a first nor a second generation. They should be regarded as, and we will call them, the 'intermediate generation'.[16]

The position of first generation Italians towards standard Italian varies considerably. The vast majority had little schooling in Italy. Most men studied only up to the end of the primary level; some had a few years of apprentice instruction after primary school. For many women also the primary school certificate remains the highest qualification, but many of them left school earlier. Their fluency in reading standard Italian is limited and their ability in writing very poor as a result of lack of formal education, further compromised by lack of practice in the original village – where such ability was neither required for community interaction, nor for work purposes. Naturally this phenomenon of semi-literacy in standard Italian, which originated in Italy, was further aggravated in the foreign environment, where needs and facilities to use standard Italian were drastically reduced. However, their oral competence in that language varies considerably according to sex, age and time of departure from Italy. We have found some people (normally men) who can fully understand, as well as express themselves, in near-standard Italian forms (regional Italian), although only in a conversational code, while types of elaborated code are still beyond their competence, but also we have found people (mainly women) to whom standard Italian is such an alien language that they cannot even understand short and simple sentences.[17]

Factors determining the degree of competence in standard Italian

The level of verbal competence in standard Italian seems entirely determined by the duration of exposure to the national language in the country of origin. The little schooling, the few functions performed in the native village in standard Italian, the irrelevance of their educational qualifications and command of the national language to the local job market, the lack of provision and facilities in the foreign environment to revive and develop the original potential communicative competence, have reduced their fluency in that language to a random individual phenomenon. As such it is ruled only by personal and casual circumstances. They can be identified in the following major variables.

Sex: Since competence in standard Italian is exclusively determined by the duration of exposure to it, men have a better command of it than women. Prior to their departure from Italy men had more opportunities to be exposed to the national language than women.[18] This is not only due to some exclusively male activities, such as property administration, business and national service, but also to some functions and roles traditionally assigned to men in the limited public occasions within the village life: contacts with the authorities, the children's school and public offices. At the time when Italian labourers left their villages in the south of Italy, women would typically live within the family circle and therefore not need any medium of communication other than the restricted family language.

FIGURE 3.1 The position of different languages in the multilingualism of Italians in Bedford

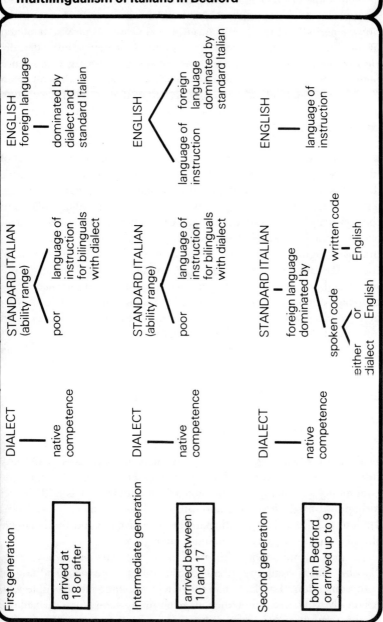

Age: Older Italian men who left their villages of origin had more opportunities to be exposed to standard Italian, and therefore to develop some verbal competence, than their younger co-villagers. The average level of education did not differ substantially between the prewar period and the very poor level of educational provision offered in some underprivileged areas of the south in the first postwar decade. Consequently the difference in levels of standard Italian competence between the younger and the older co-villagers seems to depend again on the occasional individual experience of social interaction events with an official character (e.g. national service, war, contacts with the administration and authorities).

Time of departure from Italy: Among the younger generation of immigrants, the more recent was their time of departure from Italy, the deeper is their familiarization with the national standard language. This is due to the changing conditions in southern Italian villages in the 1950s and 1960s. Greater social participation, industrialization and urban growth – which began to displace agricultural traditions – provoked significant changes in the in-group linguistic interaction of the village and moved the younger generation towards patterns of both social and family life which increasingly required competence in the national language. Consequently those immigrants who left Italy in more recent years had more opportunities to be exposed to the standard language than those who left the country some years earlier.

   However, what is more important – particularly for its influence on the language of the second generation – is that, whatever the parents' ability to understand standard Italian and their fluency in it, this language is not used as a medium of communication in the family at all.

Code-switching in the first generation

Dialect is the language spoken by first generation Italians, and many intermediate generation adults at home. For activities within the community, the language medium of communication is still dialect although it might be mixed and alternated with elements of standard Italian and English, according to the type of topic and the language they feel the other party commands better.

   In normal interaction with members of the extended family group (kinship and compari), dialect constitutes the sole medium of communication. The fact that this circle is composed of people who originally came from the same village naturally allows for a relaxed use of the community's original idiom. Conversations normally concern family events and children's experiences. Men noticeably avoid talking about work, while women do not. Code-switching into either English or standard Italian normally consists of single loan-words learnt from interacting in situations outside the community and introduced into the vocabulary of the dialect in the absence of an equivalent. Only a few examples of borrowings from everyday English vocabulary have been recorded in this type of interaction.

Stronger and more frequent elements of standard Italian are characteristic of a more significant phenomenon of code-switching in another type of interaction. This is when the conversation takes place between a member of the Italian community and a new arrival or even a northern Italian (who is never felt to be a member of the Italian community in Bedford). This type of communication involves (whenever possible and more frequently with men than women) the use chiefly of 'standard regional Italian' – subject to continuous interferences from the dialect. This is also the medium normally used in the consulate offices to obtain documents and information, or in church during a confession. However, we have seen that the exclusive use of standard Italian by the other party in these institutions often provokes problems of communication and misunderstanding: perhaps not so much in the consulate offices where a dialect-speaking member of their staff can act as an interpreter, but certainly in church where all three priests appointed come from the north of Italy.

Since the use of standard Italian is restricted to circumstances where no other medium is available for mutual comprehension, it should not be too surprising that when the use of dialect is not sufficient for communication (viz. a member of a village A in Campania with a member of a village B in Sicily) no attempt is made to use standard Italian. The base of interaction of this type is the independent use of the two different dialects.[19] Whenever the conversation involves topics that are not derived from traditions, habits and relationships within the Italian community, but instead concerns practical matters of everyday life (shopping, work, children's education, etc.) code-switching into English becomes a common practice. This is frequently heard in Italian shops, cafés, as well as in the street outside work, schools and on buses. We have noticed that this type of switching into English involves exclusively single words or phrases, expressions of approval, disapproval, advice, command, satisfaction or dissatisfaction.[20] The English utterances are made up of at most a short string of words which normally do not contain an elaborate statement, but a short comment in the form of a colloquial and informal register, which was probably previously heard and noted as one of proven meaning and effectiveness.

Multilingualism in the second generation

The positions of the three languages, Italian dialect, standard Italian and survival English, as identified in the previous section, appear to be fairly homogeneous among the first generation, resulting – as we explained – from a common social background, a uniform level of education and similar experience of life in the new environment. In the intermediate generation we found that the role and the mutual interference of each language upon the other varies considerably as a consequence of differing durations of schooling and social experience in the two countries, which produces a complex system of linguistic interference.[21] However, among the children born in Bedford of Italian parents, the second generation, definite lines can be drawn limiting the roles of the three languages, and the types of functions performed in the different behavioural situations. These functions are peculiar to the second generation. The comparison of the first and second generations' linguistic functions reveals a striking discrepancy in the language behaviour of parents and children, which also accounts for the significant cultural and emotional conflict between the generations.

In the previous section we have explained why standard Italian cannot play any role in Italian family communication. The regional dialect with its prominence as a first language, and with its position as a community language, has always been for the parents the only medium available for relaxed interaction among themselves, and of course, with the children. Therefore the Italian dialect is in every respect the first language of all children born to Italian parents in Bedford. Up to school age, such language satisfies all communicative needs between children and parents. Whether or not English is the language of social interaction in the broader context outside the family – up to school age – does not seem to affect significantly the child's communication before age 5. As a result of the first generation's in-group tendency, the opportunities available to children to be exposed to and to develop a valuable pre-school competence in English are fairly limited. Their games normally take place inside the home, rarely in the street. Playgrounds are not available in the immigrants' areas of the town and it is doubtful whether, if they were, mothers would have the time to take their children to them. Play-groups for infants are not always available, and generally Italian parents prefer the more expensive Italian Church full-day nursery to the shorter day LEA nursery school: this allows them two more hours away from home which may result in a full-time rather than a part-time job. But, in general, the parents do not like to take the infant to a public nursery.

and they prefer to make private arrangements. Sometimes it is the Italian grandmother or another woman from the same family group or village who takes care of the young children, while both parents are at work, somebody who is too old or too unfit to cope with the tough work given to Italian women. At other times it is the 'comare' herself.

The children's language development up to the age of 5 takes place in the company of parents and relatives. English may never be heard from an adult, unless relatives join the family group bringing their grown-up children. English may be heard from older siblings already attending primary or secondary school. From seven upwards, in fact, children will probably talk in English between themselves and possibly respond in English to a parent's utterance in dialect. The infant will be rather confused, but still try to understand the conversation or to follow the games of his older brothers and sisters. However, the most important source of exposure to English for a child before school age is television. The Italian child is left in front of it for several hours a day. Consequently it can be assumed that, if lack of exposure to family interaction in English cannot stimulate any productive skills in linguistic models related to functional performance, at least the intense, although passive, exposure to the television should familiarize the child with the language of the wider community. It has been noted that the child does develop some ability in discriminating and recognizing the sounds of English even at pre-school age. This ability has some tangible effects when he starts school.

From the first day of school the child of Italian parents is in the same group as his English peers. The child hears the teacher's voice: 'Sit down' 'Take your bottle of milk' 'Stop messing about' and obviously recalls the voice from the television. Perhaps he doesn't understand the speech, but gradually, taking part in the various and entertaining activities in the class-room, he learns to mimic his peers' responses, both gestures and speech. He has already learnt to discriminate and recognize the sounds of English as a result of his practice with television, he is now learning to attach meaning to phonemic sequences, which will complete his ability to decode. Over a period of one year the mental puzzle produced by passive exposure to the sounds of the television is almost entirely solved by school activities. After this period the child will gradually bring into his home well-formed English sentences of desire, question, satisfaction and dissatisfaction. Together with this repertoire of utterances of a highly imitative nature and characterized by a native-like command of the surface structures of that language, the child has learnt to attach to that medium sharply connotative and emotional values: the usefulness of a language which is the exclusive linguistic medium of interaction with the peer group (in school and playground), and a confidence in certain behaviour patterns – associated with that language – which he has recently learnt and immediately felt as more communicable and productive in the classroom and with his teachers. At this point the preliminary process establishing compartmentalized conditions as a result of the different social roles attributed to the two languages of exposure and interaction has been completed.[22]

After the four years of primary school, however sophisticated the command of dialect developed at home, however slow the child's development of literacy skills in English and poor its use as a cognitive medium, however effective the course in standard Italian at secondary school level,[23] the opposing and discrete usage of the two languages – Italian dialect and English – will be fully established in the child. The dialect will remain purely a medium of intimate and emotional interaction within the family group: a kind of family jargon. Its role is that of a speech variety related to a functional specificity, which, instead of being derived from the language of the broader context (English) happens to be governed by the roles of grammar and phonology of another language. Like all registers or speech varieties of only one language, its function is to convey more forceful and meaningful experiences not covered by more formal registers. But unlike another variety of the language of the same social context, it provides only a temporary and transitional state of bilingualism in that the linguistic competence involved is closely related to the access, the understanding, and what is more, the acceptance of values and situations related to it.

We have noticed that children tend to restrict use of the dialect almost exclusively to communication with parents, and that they prefer to use English even with their brothers and sisters or Italian friends from the same family group. Also although *'a casa mia non si parla inglese'* (there will be no English spoken in this home) is a common principle of many first generation Italians, the leading pattern of everyday conversation shows that, after a certain age (9–10), children reply in English to parents addressing them in dialect. Variations on this pattern do not depend upon children's competence in dialect, but rather upon their acceptance of the parents' habits, values and background. Consequently, at adolescence when the second generation comes to question the role of their family tradition, personal feelings and social considerations attached to the values expressed in their family language tend to question the benefit of possessing another tongue. The reactions that we have recorded show that in the case of the second generation the role of the two languages in the individual's linguistic development, and in family and social interaction, is a psychological matter.

The conflict between the two generations

The highly conservative attitude of the first generation in relation to habits and values of their original traditions, and their consequent introversion in their own community, has provoked a deep conflict with the second generation that has grown up in a mixed group and been exposed to the pressure of a wider context. It is in the area of personal and social aspirations that one can find causes of friction and conflict with the parents' tradition. This is probably due to the stronger control exercised by the family environment. In this respect children are subject to enormous pressure from home, but seem to be reluctant to reject the indigenous environment: they grow away from their parents' individual and social behaviour. Their reactions are worth considering for their psychological motives and their linguistic implications.

Reactions of the second generation and their linguistic implications

The apathetic reaction

The apathetic reaction involves a predominance in the individual of the tendency to submit to the pressure of the wider social context and accept the values of the majority group. Attainment of this goal requires that the individual rid himself of most habits, values and associations that mark him as Italian and become as completely English as possible. A clear break from his Italian background and connotations seems almost always impossible, but the apathetic reaction develops when the individual feels unable to cope with the conflicting values of the two opposing environments, and naturally slides towards acceptance of one – the one from which the pressure comes more strongly. Often the individual becomes dependent on the obsessive idea of conforming with the environment but, while declaring himself totally English, he may still retain a certain amount of Italian background and conditioning. Here the passive attitude that has made him unable to sort out his own personal conflict also prevents him from understanding the functions and the roles of the two opposing sets of values and behaviour. This attitude is that of the majority of adolescents and young second generation Italians in Bedford.

Certainly the introvert tendency of the Italian group and the total lack of facilities in this small industrial town to expand the role's repertoire in terms of the minority group's language and culture, must make the challenge of bilingualism to most second generation children a source of behavioural conflict. The linguistic outcome of this attitude is obviously a sharp tendency to monolingualism in English after a transitional state of bilingualism with the Italian dialect. This is evidenced by rejection of the learning of standard Italian in high schools recorded in areas throughout Britain, where children do not have the opportunity to benefit from formal instruction in that language at primary and middle levels.

The in-group reaction

The in-group reaction is similar to the apathetic reaction in that it represents the dominance of the tendency to approach a single one of the two incompatible goals. But in the in-group reaction, the goal is affiliation with the Italian instead of the English portion of the wider community. The individual strives primarily to identify himself with the Italian group, its traditions and aspirations and he seems to solve his conflict by a determination to please his fellow Italians (parents, relatives and kinfolk) rather than to win favour with the English. In conditions of enormous social pressure from the majority groups and the lack of significant social roles and values provided by the Italian group as a concrete and appealing alternative, their reaction develops mainly in individuals who feel close to the family group. This attitude, uncommon but still identifiable among the Italian community, accounts for the strong unity among members recorded in a few family groups in the town. In those cases unity does not mean lack of conflict between the generations, but rather testifies to an attempt to find refuge in the family's values and habits as an alternative to those observed and experienced in the indigenous group. Limited facilities and varieties of social interaction in this small and rapidly industrialized town, and severely restricted social mobility between classes are probably the main sources of frustration and disappointment for some second generation young people. They see a return into the family group as the only available escape.

These cases represent the perpetuation of Italian community life and language among the second generation group in Bedford. Also in these cases one can observe an extension of the transitional state of bilingualism (English and Italian dialect) analysed in younger children in the previous section. Unlike individuals developing an apathetic reaction, they are exposed to and accept two sets of 'compartmentalized' roles and the linguistic repertoires related to them.[24] However, since the social roles requested from English are restricted purely to survival functions (work and occasional contacts outside the community) by a personal choice, the chances that these individuals will acquire new roles in that medium and therefore develop linguistic and social emancipation remain limited.

The rebel reaction

The last major attitude among the second generation recorded in Bedford can be defined as the rebel reaction, but it represents the position of only a few young people. Unlike the previous reaction, the individuals who have been seen developing a rebel attitude towards both communities have not indulged in the temptation to escape either group to gain favour and security in the other. Here the conflicting values attributed to the two communities have produced in them a strong interest in investigating both, for their personal and social implications. In consequence they have made an attempt to approach and understand the two 'compartmentalized' sets of roles and values by means of personal experience, refusing the conflicting presentation of them provided by either group. These individuals are found among those who benefited from close parental guidance, stronger motivation in their studies, from personal contacts with Italy and from higher education. In particular one compartment that undoubtedly has favoured awareness of their cultural conflict has been access to new sets of role repertoires related to the language of their parents, the national standard language of their country of origin and the cultural values expressed there. The acquisition of these sets of linguistic and role repertoires has been witnessed so far among those of the second generation exposed to functions of social interaction in Italian, in Italy; certainly not those who have attended evening classes in Italian in Bedford. This is particularly relevant, since it shows that voluntary language provision offered outside the school, with limited resources by community organizations, cannot produce among the second generation an awareness and understanding of sets of role and value repertoires differing from those developed and provided by the families themselves. Such provision does not appear to be stimulating, and it seldom succeeds in helping the children overcome negative associations in their over-all social and linguistic behaviour.

The rebel's reaction is characterized by the awareness of such conflicting associations, generated and presented by both groups. As such it shows an understanding, developed in Italy or outside the community in Bedford (e.g. in higher education), of the restricted role repertoires performed in the group by the members of the community as well as parents. Consequently the reaction to the influence of either ethnic group develops when second generation individuals become capable of considering and evaluating from outside the background and the role of their families. And this seems to be achieved when they succeed in placing them in a wider social and linguistic context: the social context that accounts for the parents' uprooting, and their opposition to the new environment; and the linguistic context that clarifies the relationship between inadequate values and restricted linguistic repertoires, as developed by the community language. Such awareness involves, and indeed seems to require, a deep familiarization with Italian life and society as well as literacy and full command of standard Italian.

In consequence, it produces bilingual individuals who, apart from the dialect spoken at home, can command and function equally well both in English and the national language of their parents' country of origin. Only very few such cases have been found in Bedford and this should lead educationists to a reconsideration and evaluation of the linguistic provision made available to children in such communities.[25]

Notes

1 Most sections of this chapter have appeared in 'Semilingualism, Diglossia and Bilingualism', *Lingua e contesto* **4**, 1979, Atlantica Editrice, Manfredonia. The author gratefully acknowledges permission to republish.

2 A detailed analysis of different viewpoints on the teaching of the mother tongue to children of migrant workers in Britain, with particular reference to the Italian group, is proposed in Tosi (1978).

3 For discussion on the notion of semilingualism or semibilingualism see the survey articles by Swain and Cummins (1979) and by Tosi (1979b).

4 Mother tongue classes in the curriculum are offered in pilot projects in Bradford and Bedfordshire. The first scheme is funded by the Department of Education and Science, and the second by the European Commission.

5 An historical view of the political development of and a review of the academic discussion about mother tongue teaching to migrants' children in Europe, with full bibliographical references, can be found in Tosi (1979b).

6 See also Pellegrini (1960), (1962), (1974).

7 An experiment of 'guided standardization' in Italian classes for children bilingual in English and Campano dialect is reported in 'Bilinguismo, transfert e interferenze', a paper given at the Conference on 'Linguistica Contrastiva', Asti, May 1979. See Tosi (forthcoming 1).

8 See also 'The Relationship between Learning Processes and Teaching Methods in Developing Migrants' Children Bilingual Literacy', Tosi (forthcoming 3).

9 It might be useful to mention here the important 'Linguistic Minorities Project'. This project is based at the Institute of Education, London University, and is funded by the Department of Education and Science. It has a three years' duration and started in September 1979 under the direction of Dr Verity Saifullah Khan.

10 Further information on the settlement of southern Italians in Bedford is available in 'Little Italy in Bedford' (*The Times* 1960); 'Bilingualism in Bedford' (Walker 1963); 'Napoli, Bedfordshire' (Barr 1974); 'The Italian Connection' (King 1977). Among

these articles and reports, the paper by King provides by far the best insight into the problems of adjustment of southern Italians in Bedford. The book *The Unmelting Pot* (Brown 1970), which contains also a section on southern Italians, offers an outline of the social and cultural conditions of all ethnic minority groups in Bedford. The section on the Italians focuses particularly upon the conflict between generations. A recent history of the formation of the Italian community, concerned particularly with the distinction between migrants and immigrants, is reported in Tosi (1979a).

11   For data and statistical information on Italian immigration to Britain see *The Invisible Immigrants* (Runnymede 1972) and *Linguistic Minorities in Britain* (Runnymede 1976, 1978). The majority of information contained in these publications is drawn from data included in the Census of 1971 and is no longer relevant. See also Sponza (ed.) (1979).

12   Both quotations are taken from Barr (1974).

13   For life conditions of southern Italians in immigrant communities see Child (1943), a study that focuses upon the social adjustment and the conflict between generations in a community of southern Italians living in New Haven, Connecticut; see also Boissevain (1971).

14   'Compare' (godfather) and 'comare' (godmother), which appears later in the paper, are two very protective and influential figures in the life of southern Italian families and in the upbringing of their children.

15   In this paper the term 'dialect' refers to the Italian socio-linguistic context, where the linguistic varieties represent social and linguistic situations different from those normally described by the term 'dialect' in use in English-speaking countries. As Trumper (1977) has pointed out, in anglophone countries the term 'dialects', if not defined otherwise, described the complex social variations of one language, which present structural similarities with the standard code, to the point that makes possible a fairly high degree of mutual comprehension between speakers. Such definition is certainly not adequate for the complex Italian situation, as the author quoted has emphasized. For further clarification see also Lepschy and Lepschy (1977).

16   The age range defining the boundaries of the area called 'intermediate generation' is by no means rigid. In fact even those immigrants who were born in Italy and migrated in their early childhood (up to 10) are, literally speaking, first generation themselves. However it was found that those subjects who arrived in the host country as children and completed all or most of their education in the new country, share many of their linguistic and cultural features with the second generation. But those who arrived from 10 upwards, and spend more than just the primary education period in Italian schools, present linguistic and psychological traits remarkably different from the second generation. Accordingly, I have identified the area of this immigrant population – which I have called the 'intermediate generation' – within the limits of the age corresponding to the beginning of the middle school (approximately 10 years old) up to the age when a young man or woman is still likely to be attending school or further education courses. The intermediate generation is made up of immigrants born in the country of origin but their exposure to the language and the culture in the new country, both in everyday life and in formal education, results in the development of some of the features of a second generation. Consequently they may be distinguished from the first generation, although they are not fully participant in the environmental conditions of the second generation.

17   The classic study on the position of dialects in Italian society is *Storia linguistica dell'Italia unita* by De Mauro (1963). A more recent socio-linguistic review on

bilingualism in Italy presented with Fishman's categories is given by Mioni (1975) 'Per una sociolinguistica italiana: note di un non sociologo' and also in Mioni (1979) 'La situazione sociolinguistica italiana: lingua, dialetti, italiani regionali'.

18   This is a particular southern not general Italian phenomenon. In the south of Italy males lead in both 'overt prestige' and 'covert prestige', see Trumper (in press), contrary to the general American and European norm where women lead in 'overt prestige', men in 'covert prestige'. See Labov (1972) and Trudgill (1974).

19   Many phonetic–phonological changes affecting dialect systems of immigrants from Sicily and Molise seem to suggest the development of *koine* phenomena in the speech of southern Italians in Bedford, with predominant influence of the Campano–Irpino variety. However, the cases observed had not been sufficiently investigated by the time this paper was completed to allow for a full assessment of the phenomenon.

20   See 'Aspetti cross-culturali dell'interferenza morfosemantica nel bilinguismo etnico' Tosi (forthcoming 2).

21   The cases of linguistic change and interference phenomena observed among the 'intermediate generation' as a result of the different duration of exposure to the different languages, as well as the different duration of formal education in the two countries, suggest the existence of a very large number of variables. Not having sufficient records available, I have not attempted to organize those variables in a model in this paper, since the assessment of the factors underlying these linguistic changes would have taken me far beyond the scope of the present study.

22   An overview of the factor related to the conflict psychological state in children of immigrants exposed to two languages and their implications at a linguistic and cultural level is given in Lewis (1970).

23   On the organization of courses run by the Italian Authorities outside the curriculum as well as provision for Italian as a foreign language offered by LEAs in the curriculum to children of immigrants, see Tosi (1978).

24   The identification of roles and linguistic repertoires and their applicability in a multilingual context are derived from Fishman (1967).

25   Problems, policies and perspectives of developing children of migrants' mother tongue in a foreign environment, are analysed in two interesting reports by Skutnabb-Kangas (1976) and Toukomaa and Skutnabb-Kangas (1977).

4

Language and Learning:
Intervention and the Child at Home

MAURICE CHAZAN

Over the past two decades or so, much has been said and written about
the importance of the home in the child's development, educational
progress and adjustment to school. Considerable importance too has
been attached to the verbal interaction between the parents (especially
the mother) and the child in influencing early language acquisition and
in preparing the child for the linguistic demands of the school. There is
now a considerable research literature on the relationship between
stimulation in the home, development and learning. Surprisingly,
however, the literature on intervention in the home is very sparse, and,
in fact, when we consider action in the United Kingdom, this too has
been extremely limited – particularly as far as monitored experiments
are concerned. We are still in the early stages of considering what kinds
of intervention in the home, if any, are appropriate. It might be useful,
therefore, for me to attempt an overview of the present situation, as an
introduction to discussion.

I should like to consider 'intervention in the home' under five
headings:

1   Education and preparation for parenthood
2   The role of television
3   Home-based projects for 'disadvantaged' children
4   Home-based projects for handicapped children
5   Home–school liaison

I shall be dealing mainly with intervention relating to young children,
and I shall do my best to bear in mind that we are focusing our
attention on language, although it is not easy to separate concern with
language development from more general issues.

1   Education and Preparation for Parenthood

In the USA systematic efforts in parent education began over ninety years ago and have continued vigorously ever since (Brim 1965; Auerbach (1968). In the United Kingdom, parent education has been approached much more cautiously; it does not exist here in a highly organized form, nor does there seem to be a strong demand for it. While it is true that social changes affecting the family as an institution are forcing parents into greater consciousness of their child-rearing practices, attitudes towards education for parenthood are still rather casual in Britain. In the past, advice has been sought by parents mainly over the physical care of children and in times of crisis rather than over wider aspects of the parental role. It is the parents of physically and mentally handicapped children, rather than other parents, who perceive and voice a need for help in bringing up their children.

However, evidence from our Compensatory Education Project (Chazan *et al.* 1976) suggests that many parents from varying socio-economic backgrounds would respond to advice on aspects of child rearing if this were readily available, and there is now increasing support from many quarters for a more systematic approach to parent education (Chazan 1978). The Bullock Report (Department of Education and Science 1975) put considerable emphasis on the need to help parents to understand the process of language development in their children and to take part in it. The Bullock Committee was very much in sympathy with the principle of introducing secondary school pupils to language growth in young children, and had come across excellent courses in parenthood in many schools. The Committee felt that, in schools, the language development of young children should be set in the wider context of human language rather than be seen as part of a course on personal preparation for parenthood. They advocated the use of films, demonstrations and discussions as well as practical experience in order to bring about an awareness of the adult's role in the young child's linguistic and cognitive development. Such an approach would include a study of the linguistic aspects of relationships, of the questions children ask, and of the value of discussion and explanation in controlling a child's behaviour as against simple prohibition. The Bullock Committee, too, was in favour of controlled contact between secondary school pupils and nursery and infant schools.

After school, the Bullock Committee saw the most productive point at which to introduce the subject of the language development of the young child to be when young married couples are about to become parents: at this stage language can be placed in the context of child care, in which it can be shown to have an important place. The problems in doing this were acknowledged – problems of space, facilities, time, finance and staffing (e.g. of speech therapists). Nevertheless, '. . . it is our central contention, and there is ample evidence from research to support it, that attention to language problems comes too late. The education process must be started earlier if the language deficiencies we have described are to be reduced. The difficulties of implementing such a policy at the ante-natal stage must not be allowed to obscure the need for one' (Bullock Report, p. 58).

A variety of approaches to parents are possible at the time they are bringing up children – home-visiting (seen up to now as mainly applicable to disadvantaged and handicapped children, but all parents are, for example, on health visitors' lists); discussion groups; written material; radio and television programmes; and courses (e.g. those provided by the Open University). Most parents are likely to respond to approaches that are personal and specific rather than impersonal and general, though the mass media have a valuable part to play in education for parenthood.

So far I have talked mainly about approaches to educating parents, but the question remains whether it is worthwhile spending a lot of time and money on parent education. Resistance to systematic education for parenthood is still to be met, for a variety of reasons, e.g.

   i.   Some people consider that bringing up children is a 'natural' function that is best carried out without interference from experts: increasing professional instruction may lead parents to become more knowledgeable, perhaps, but less warm and spontaneous in their relationships with their children. Preoccupation with language development, for example, could result in parents being stilted and artificial in talking to their children.

  ii.   Telling or even showing parents what they ought to do does not mean that they will be able to put advice into practice.

 iii.   Parents may receive conflicting advice from different sources and become confused; they may misunderstand or distort the implications of certain viewpoints. They may get the impression, through systematic courses in parenthood, that there is one right way of bringing up children.

Barbara Tizard (1974a), reviewing research on parent education programmes related to pre-school children, cautions that we have very little knowledge at even the most superficial level about the learning environment of young children at home, and about which aspects of their environment are significant for later scholastic achievement. In her view, much of the thinking about parent education seems both psychologically and sociologically simplistic: we are increasingly coming to understand that what the child learns, and how he learns it, depends to an extent on the characteristics of the communication system within the family. I would agree with this, but on balance I think that the case for more systematic parent education programmes is a powerful one, as long as such programmes are prepared with very great care and adequately monitored.

2 The Role of Television

It is all too easy to blame television for many of the ills of modern society, but we need to face the facts that nearly every home – even in socially deprived areas – has a television set; that, in the case of young children at home, television has a great appeal in that it is highly attractive and novel, with no real competition most of the time; and that young children learn much from watching television, even if the learning includes a great deal of knowledge that parents do not want their children to acquire. Television provides opportunities for mother–child interaction and dialogue – opportunities that our Swansea-based inquiries showed were taken up in only a minority of cases. In only about a third of 120 families involved in our study did the mother use the chance to extend the child's experience and language by sharing his TV watching in a very active way; in most cases, the mother took only a slight interest in the child's viewing (Chazan *et al*. 1971).

The American TV programme *Sesame Street*, designed specifically for pre-school children, has aroused a great deal of interest in Britain and other countries, and is still being shown on some ITV networks. Its main feature is the very precise statement of the instructional goals that has guided its production (Ball and Bogatz 1970; Bogatz and Ball 1971). The development of language plays an important part in *Sesame Street*, which aims at teaching, *inter alia*, relational concepts, classification, ordering and reasoning at the appropriate level. The evaluation of the programme undertaken by the Educational Testing Service in the USA suggested that all types of viewers aged 3 to 5 years gained from watching – disadvantaged frequent viewers gained as much as advantaged frequent viewers. Monitoring in Britain by the Independent Television Authority showed that reactions to *Sesame Street* were very varied, the American flavour of the material tending to be a drawback in the general acceptability of the programmes (ITA Report 1971). However, many lessons can be learnt from *Sesame Street* by the producers of pre-school programmes as well as by the children themselves, who tend to enjoy watching it. More resources ought to be put into television for young children.

Television (and indeed radio) also makes a considerable contribution to parent education through its programmes about children. I do not think, however, that the full potential of the mass media is being exploited by educationists, who ought to become far more involved in television than they are at present.

3   Home-based Projects for 'Disadvantaged' Children

Parental involvement has for long been seen as an essential ingredient in compensatory programmes for socially disadvantaged children, on the grounds that

 i.   the family is the major socializing influence on the child;
 ii. nursery schooling plays only a small part in the child's life;
 iii. liaison between home and school helps to ensure continuity in children's experience.

Many different approaches have been adopted to parental involvement – group meetings, active participation of parents in educational programmes, training parents to make imaginative use of materials to stimulate the child, book library and toy library schemes, and home-visiting. Home-based parent education has been regarded by some as being a particularly effective strategy, inasmuch as many parents, for a variety of reasons, are unwilling or unable to participate in activities arranged for them outside the home. Further, it is argued that it is appropriate to involve parents on an individual basis, and that home-visiting can reach children well before they are of nursery school age.

USA

Early home-based programmes in the USA tended to focus directly on the child rather than on the parents. For example, Schaefer (1972) instituted a programme in Washington in which one hour's home 'instruction' was provided daily for twenty-four infants from the ages of 15 months to 3 years. This programme failed to show any significant gains, though these were assessed in terms of changes in IQ – a very doubtful procedure, especially at this age. However, Levenstein (1970) in New York, using 'toy demonstrators' to visit homes twice weekly for thirty minutes, with varied kits of books and play materials, aimed at stimulating interaction between mother and child. IQ gains between 10 and 20 points were recorded, and were maintained for some time after the programme ceased.

One of the best-structured home-based programmes in the USA has been the Florida Parent Education programme (Gordon 1968, 1973, 1975). The main aim of this programme was to teach the mother a set of specific, sequential tests to use with her infant, beginning at 3 months and continuing to 2 years. The earliest years of life were considered critical, and the main goals were

   i. the development of a career programme for disadvantaged women to serve as parent-educators and child development workers;

  ii. the education of mothers in specific techniques for cognitive and verbal stimulation accompanying a warm interpersonal relationship; and

 iii. providing infants with an environment conducive to effective growth.

The Piagetian view of the importance of the sensori-motor period in the intellectual development of the child was the basis for the cognitive tasks, and the language programme was based on Bernstein's work, aiming to present the mother with a model of a more elaborate language code than she might otherwise use. The programme involved the training of mothers from the same social class as the mothers to be helped; home visits once weekly for about an hour, when specific tasks were presented for the mother to learn, through demonstration and role-playing; and teaching the parent-educators to make toys from free or inexpensive materials and to pass on these skills to the mothers.

In this as in most other projects, difficulties were encountered in establishing and maintaining relationships with some families, especially those who were disorganized and under great pressure simply to maintain life itself. However, the use of the parent-educator rather than a professional social worker helped greatly in the establishment of rapport and in reducing defensiveness and hostility. The Florida programme is said to have had long-term beneficial effects, with only 1 per cent of the 200 children having to be referred to special education classes, as compared with 30 per cent in similar children not participating (Lewin 1977).

Bronfenbrenner (1974a) reviewed nine parent–child intervention studies focusing simultaneously on parent (almost exclusively the mother) and child as the targets of intervention, and concluded that children who were involved in an intensive programme of parent intervention during and, especially, prior to their enrolment in pre school or school, achieved greater and more enduring gains in the group programme. Parent intervention was of benefit not only for the target child but also for his younger siblings, and it influenced the attitudes of the mother both to the child and to herself as a competent person capable of improving her own situation. The key elements of the intervention were the involvement of parent and child in verbal interaction round a cognitively challenging task and the existence of a mutual and enduring emotional attachment between child and adult.

However, along with its advantages, parent intervention appears to have serious limitations in terms of its applicability to and effectiveness with families in the lowest extreme of the socio-economic distribution. Bronfenbrenner therefore advocates intervention at the 'ecological level' – effecting radical changes in the immediate environment of the family. Intervention of this more radical kind (though not as comprehensive as Bronfenbrenner has in mind) was attempted by Heber and Garber (1975) at Milwaukee. In this project, forty low-income families with new-born infants and where the mothers were of low intelligence were divided into experimental and control groups. The programme provided adult education and occupational training for the mothers and structured tutoring for the infants – initially at home and later at a full-time day-care centre. Both groups of children developed along similar lines for the first fourteen months, but by sixty-six months a mean difference in IQ of 30 points was found between the groups, the average for the experimental group being 124; there was a 1–1½ years difference in language development. The intervention ceased at age 6, when the children entered the first grade. The mean IQ of the experimental group had by then declined to 106, though it was still higher than the controls, and no differences between the groups were recorded in respect of reading abilities. Clarke and Clarke (1976) suggest that either

   i. the intervention was insufficiently lengthy to enable the children, in their still rather adverse home and school contexts, to maintain their degree of gain – which hypothesis they favour; or

   ii. the early acceleration of development had merely enabled the children to reach their genetic limits earlier, and that these limits will progressively exercise constraints upon development, reflected in decelerating growth.

Page (1972) has also raised a number of questions and doubts about the project.

On the whole, the results of educational home-visiting projects in the USA should encourage us to experiment with programmes of this kind here, although certain features of the American schemes are not easily incorporated into practice in this country, e.g. the use of 'disadvantaged' mothers as home-educators or payment to mothers willing to be helped through home-visiting.

United Kingdom

Since 1970, when educational home-visiting was first introduced into the United Kingdom as part of the EPA action-research project in the West Riding, a number of home-based schemes have been launched here, with the main objectives of (1) raising the morale and self-esteem of the mother, and (2) helping parents to foster the child's linguistic, social and motor development. Some schemes have been inaugurated by local education authorities, using professionals (usually teachers or health visitors), some are undertaken by voluntary agencies (National Children's Bureau 1977 a and b).

In general, the educational visitors pay regular weekly visits to the home, lasting about an hour, taking toys, games and books. They tend to concentrate on helping mothers to develop specific skills in interacting with their children (mainly aged 18 months to 4 years). Most school-based programmes visit families within a school catchment area rather than select a particularly 'deprived' population, to avoid possible stigma and labelling, but independent bodies tend to work with multi-problem families.

It is not easy to assess the effectiveness of home-visiting programmes, especially as very young children are involved, and evaluation studies have not been numerous (Woodhead 1976). However, a controlled study was undertaken as part of the EPA Area Project in the West Riding of Yorkshire, involving home visits over a year to twenty-five children aged between 18 months and 2 years (Smith 1975; Armstrong 1975). The need for help with language development soon became obvious – mothers would often anticipate the child's needs, and the child's language was often restricted, particularly where there were two young children at home all day. The smaller and less developed children were treated like babies because they looked like babies, and fewer demands were made on them. Very few of the children had used 'learning' toys by 21 months, but they soon found real pleasure in discovering new materials. On the basis of varied assessment techniques, the experimental group emerged as more vocal, imaginative and sociable. More important, however, than the change in test performance was the change in the mothers' attitudes to the children's development and their own role. None of them had initially seen themselves as playing a vital role in their children's intellectual development, but once the 'experimental' mothers began to join in the children's activities, they saw how much they were teaching them and they wanted to find out how they could help further. The child's obvious pleasure in what they were doing was the main factor in making the parents react favourably. Some of the parents were afraid of teachers and therefore not keen to approach schools. These parents could easily be labelled as 'apathetic' or 'not interested', but their enthusiasm could be aroused with encouragement.

Donachy (1972, 1976) has also carried out controlled studies on mother–child interaction. His initial inquiry in Renfrewshire was designed to test the hypothesis that the general intellectual and linguistic competence of 'culturally deprived' pre-school children would rise significantly when they had been exposed to a home-based programme which enhanced verbal interaction between the children and their mothers. He compared an experimental group of nine children with two control groups (each of nine children), all meeting criteria of 'cultural deprivation' on the Stanford-Binet Intelligence scale and the Reynell Development Language scales, before and after the exposure of the experimental group to six months of weekly home sessions, during which the home visitors used toys and books to stimulate verbal interaction between mother and child. To take account of a possible Hawthorne effect, one control group received weekly visits and non-experimental gifts from the home visitors, while the other control group received no intervention between tests. The experimental group's gains were significantly greater than those of the other group in IQ but not in language.

In a subsequent study, forty-eight children aged 3 and 4 years receiving a four-month programme administered by mothers at home and organized through the local primary school or nursery were compared with forty-eight children receiving either normal nursery schooling or no intervention between tests. Children involved in the parent programme made significant gains on the Stanford-Binet scale and on the Reynell Language scales; those receiving nursery enrichment, but no parent programme, made significant gains on the Stanford-Binet, but not on the Reynell scales; while the children receiving no intervention between tests made no significant gains on either measure.

Donachy comments that

i.   although mothers read to their children before the programme, with guidance they involved the children much more in such activity;

ii. the mothers became more aware of natural teaching opportunities in the ordinary routines of the day;

iii. the teachers involved found contact with parents much easier and more valuable than they anticipated;

iv. perhaps more important than the measured gains which might not last, were the gains in relationships.

While both the West Riding and the Renfrewshire home-visiting projects were limited in scope and short-term, their results are encouraging and suggest that such projects could well be extended. As Donachy states, we have hardly begun to explore the potential of pre-school children.

4 Home-based Projects for Handicapped Children

I shall deal only briefly with home-based projects for handicapped children – who present specific and often major problems as far as language is concerned – as I have reviewed the field elsewhere (Chazan 1979). I would like, however, to make a few points about intervention in the home as far as handicapped children and language are concerned:

   i.   Whatever the handicap – physical, mental or emotional – retardation in language development (particularly expressive) is frequently found.

   ii. Children with delayed language development need early help if this is to be effective.

   iii. Parents become very anxious about delayed language development, and many of them actively seek help. Their needs are not always met, but they are especially appreciative of help given by speech therapists when available.

   iv. The one-to-one relationship between mother and child provides an excellent basis for language development, and many parents very much want to do something constructive themselves for their children rather than sit back and wait for outside help.

A variety of projects have been set up to help parents to acquire skills in fostering language development where this is delayed or non-existent. In the main, help has been provided through the dissemination of literature (which has limited value without personal support and guidance as a back-up); workshops, mostly employing a behaviour modification approach (O'Dell 1974; Cunningham 1975; Jeffree and McConkey 1976 a and b); and home-visiting schemes.

The home-visiting approach can be illustrated by reference to the Portage Early Education Project (Bluma *et al.* 1976), devised in the USA and now being used in several areas in Britain. The Portage programme is designed to help children functioning about one year or more below their age level in physical, self-help, social, cognitive or communication skills. If the child is considered eligible for the scheme, the home teacher selects each week, with the aid of the parent, one or two skills for mastery.

Once a skill is chosen, the home teacher refers to the Portage Curriculum Guide, which consists of a box containing a card for each step on the developmental checklist used to obtain a baseline behavioural profile of the child (there are ninety-nine cards in the language section). Each card suggests activities that are likely to be helpful in teaching the specific skill in question; these serve as a starting point helping teacher and parent to develop their ideas. The home teacher plans and writes up one or two 'activity charts' for the coming week. After a week, she returns to evaluate the child's progress by taking post-baseline data, and makes further suggestions in the light of her findings. In addition to her educational function, the home teacher tends to become involved in discussing family problems with the parents and in advising them where to seek appropriate help. An evaluation of the Portage programme has been carried out in Britain by the Wessex Health Care Evaluation Research Team, who found the approach to be of value and also acceptable to the mothers involved, though they suggest that a number of changes might be made within the total package (Smith *et al.* 1977).

5   Home–School Liaison

I should like to conclude with a brief reference to the role of the school in home-based intervention projects. I have already mentioned Donachy's emphasis on the importance of linking intervention in the home with nursery and infant schools rather than this being seen as a separate operation – a view that I would strongly support. In the case of language programmes, it is clearly desirable that there should be collaboration between parents, home educators and the school over both the content of programmes and the approaches to be used. Not only does such collaboration help to ensure consistency and continuity of approach, but, as Donachy found, parents and teachers come to understand each other much better.

Liaison between home and school is not always easy to promote, and formidable barriers may exist that prevent harmonious and constructive relationships between teachers and parents. Some teachers may lack confidence in relating to parents, or simply not recognize collaboration with parents as a part of their work. While many parents have a keen, or at least a mild, interest in co-operation with teachers, some are quite content to leave education entirely to the school, and some have such severe personal problems that they are unable to find time or energy for educational concerns (Chazan *et al.* 1976). Nevertheless, promoters of home-visiting schemes would do well to encourage nursery and infant schools to participate in their work, even if children not yet at school are the only ones to be involved.

5

Language in Its Social Context and the Role of Educational Home Visitors

JOHN RAVEN

The main objective of this paper is to summarize some of the results of an evaluation of an Educational Home Visiting scheme (Raven 1980). Before turning to the data, however, something must be said about the Home Visiting scheme itself (McCail 1981).

The scheme, which was brought into being in the Lothian Region of Scotland by Ian MacFadyen, had its roots in a number of research traditions. The first of these was the Plowden (1966), Douglas (1964), National Children's Bureau (Davie *et al.* 1972) and Coleman (1966) work, which showed that many children seemed to do less well at school than their measured intelligence predicted.

The second was the widely held, if erroneous, view, promulgated by Peaker (1967, 1971), Coleman (1966), and Davé (1963) that some two-thirds of the variance in school performance was attributable to home background.

The third was the equally widely held view that this variance in cognitive/academic ability was well established by the time the child was 5 and was, therefore, in the light of the two previous conclusions, a result of something to do with early experience in the home and, in particular, with language experience.

The fourth was Bronfenbrenner's (1975) review of the research literature on intervention programmes, which suggested that their effects were less likely to 'wash out' if the mother could be involved directly in the intervention herself. This suggested to Ian MacFadyen that he focus on strategies that had an affinity with those of Levenstein (1970, 1972, 1975) and those adopted in the Dublin project (Kellaghan 1977; Kellaghan and Archer 1973 and 1975).

The scheme began with a single Educational Home Visitor (EHV) attached to a nursery school that was specifically intended to promote

parental involvement. At the end of the year Ian MacFadyen interviewed many of the parents involved and was so impressed by the
result that he arranged for the number of Educational Home Visitors to
be increased to six on an experimental basis, and for an independent
evaluation to be carried out by the Scottish Council for Research in
Education with funds from the Scottish Education Department. These
home visitors, who were all trained teachers, were appointed to the
staffs of schools in six 'deprived' areas, and paid by the Lothian
Regional Council. Their brief was, in the context of the perspectives
that have been summarized earlier, to work with 2- to 3-year-old
children in their parents' presence for about one hour a week. The
length of time the visiting would be kept up was left open, but has
turned out to be about nine months on average. The objective of the
weekly visits was to encourage the mothers to play a more active role in
promoting the educational development of their children. It was
suggested that the Educational Home Visitor should begin by involving
the child in activities in which language was used to extend his
imagination, and then seek to involve the mother in such activities.
However, it was envisaged from the start that, as the home visitors
became more comfortable in their new role, these activities would be
extended to include encouraging the mother to take a more active role
in relation to the formal educational system and to participate in
activities that would lead her to become more confident and outgoing.
It was envisaged that this would in turn influence the development of
her children.

The home visitors each visited about ten families per week. Thus,
about 180 families were visited in the first two years of operation. This
makes the project one of the largest of its kind in the world.

The EHVs were encouraged to exercise their professional judgement
as to how best to interpret the general guidelines that have been
summarized, and how to relate them to the needs of individual families,
schools and communities. It was recognized that this would lead to
considerable variance between the home visitors, and an attempt was
made to select visitors who, while open to feedback, would have
sufficient confidence in their own judgement not to require continual
reassurance or direction.

The extent of the variance that did occur will be documented later,
but a hint may be given here by saying that the first visitor 'agonized'
over the Dublin and Levenstein approaches but found that they 'left
her cold'. She discussed with her head teacher whether she should tell
MacFadyen this and they decided not to do so. This fact will, of course,
horrify anyone brought up in an academic climate that emphasizes tidy

psychological experiments. But, it appears, it is our conception of an experiment that is wrong – not this project.

It is because there was so much variance between the EHVs that we had to spend such a lot of time studying the activities actually under-taken by the EHVs – instead of assuming that they were doing what the administrator said they were doing. What is staggering is that, despite widespread 'evaluation' of such programmes in the United States, no instruments suited to the task of assessing the processes of home-visiting actually exist. If one does not know what it is that one is assessing the effects of, how can *any* useful conclusions be drawn from any of the studies?

Selection of Families

Most, but not all, of the families picked out by the schools, social workers, or health visitors were 'deprived' or 'problem' families who were selected because it was thought that they would 'benefit' in some way from the project. From the start it was made plain that it was legitimate to select families because the expected benefit was social. Despite its location in deprived areas, and its focus on 'families who might benefit', the EHVs were given explicit instructions to avoid families in which social problems were so severe that they would prevent them focusing on the educational activities that lay at the heart of the project. Thus the families who were 'most likely to benefit' were clearly not necessarily the most 'needy'. Despite this instruction, the EHVs have, in practice, found that they had a serious dilemma about whether they should work with the most 'needy' or the 'most responsive' families.

As the study has progressed these social problems, the mother's ability deficits, her isolation, and her inability to get satisfactory treatment from the social services, have come to be seen as more and more central to the problems the EHVs are trying to tackle. Although one of the Educational Home Visitors did manage to stand out against this for about two years, she became the most anxious about her inability to influence the children's cognitive development, and has now capitulated to the view that isolation and depression are central to the mother's unwillingness to become involved in the activities she is trying to encourage. However, the fact that she was able to stand out against this position for so long shows that it *is* possible for home visitors to do as Levenstein and MacFadyen suggest and not become involved in the mother's problem.

The Evaluation

The evaluation was set up as a one-man two-year project. It was set up as a 'descriptive' or 'illuminative' (rather than as a statistical) study, although it was intended that some questionnaire and test data should be collected. It was intended to monitor the development in the EHVs' understanding of their task, and monitor the impact of the project on the schools concerned, the subsequent development of their children, and the wider communities in which the home-visiting took place. It was also intended to set the project in the context of other home-visiting projects in Britain and in the United States and, by doing so, to assess what the long-term effects of the Lothian Project were likely to be.

Despite the general agreement that evaluation should be 'illuminative' and 'descriptive' rather than statistical, the ambiguity of these terms, the desired breadth of the evaluation, and a level of funding that did not provide for other research back-up, made for continuous unease about the evaluation. This unease was exacerbated by the administrator's desire for 'hard' data on the effectiveness of the programme. Initially, he had seen the evaluation as consisting solely of the administration of IQ tests to the children. Having been convinced that the prior task was to examine the impact of the programme on the parents, he repeatedly asked what methods were being used to assess that impact, and the context of his question implied that he had never fully accepted the 'illuminative' evaluation model.

The author joined the project because he saw it as an opportunity to develop the methodology required to evaluate programmes of this sort. At the time there seemed to him to be no way in which a satisfactory evaluation study could be carried out with the resources currently allocated to it, but both the project and the evaluation were set up in such a way as to imply continuity of funding and it was expected that, in the longer term, it *would* be possible to do a satisfactory job of evaluating the project.

In point of fact it rapidly became clear that there were a large number of questions that could be tackled through a formal evaluation exercise if funds could be obtained. It also became clear that the funds to develop relevant questionnaires and collect *background* data from the areas in which the home-visiting was taking place might be obtained under the Job Creation Programme, although these funds would cover only inexperienced – and changing – personnel.

The Home-Visiting

There are, in the literature, some fifteen possible, theoretically and practically based, interpretations of what activities might be implied by the phrase 'encouraging parents to play a more active part in promoting the educational development of their children'. Many of these are, in varying degrees, represented within the activities of all the EHVs.

However, despite the fact that all the EHVs draw on a common pool of activities, four styles of home-visiting may be discerned within the project. Only three of these will be discussed here because the fourth is a style developed by a home visitor who works with handicapped children.

The styles that are described below are neither 'pure' nor 'ideal types'. The descriptions leave many things out, and none of the EHVs would claim to do all of the things that are included under any one heading. The sketches simply serve to indicate the sort of variation found within the scheme. To avoid any misunderstanding it should be mentioned that, although only six home visitors have been at work at any one time, owing to two retirements, eight home visitors have in fact been associated with the scheme up to the time at which the evaluation ceased. The number of EHVs at work has subsequently increased to fifteen.

Style 1

Style 1 seems to encompass the following components:
  i.   An emphasis on teaching particular concepts: colours, relation-ships, names of objects. (Note the implicit theory of 'cognitive development'. As Bereiter and Engelmann (1966) assert, this view holds that the ability to think clearly is dependent on having relevant constructs available.)
  ii. An emphasis on teaching a 'cognitive skill' – such as how to pay attention to shapes, to the lines on bits of jigsaws, etc. The cognitive skill behind these might be described as the skill of observing, reasoning, listening or analysing. This emphasis is of course, compatible with a theory very different from that of Bereiter and Engelmann. This theory holds that the development of vocabulary, constructs, parts of speech, tenses of verbs and linguistic structure is dependent on the prior development of the ability to perceive and think clearly, since these abilities are essential to discern the complex structure of language, which no parent or teacher is in a position to teach children explicitly (Spearman 1927; MacNamara 1972).
  iii. A 'teacherish' style in interaction making extensive use of closed questions with the right or wrong answers.

iv. An emphasis on encouraging parents to adopt discipline by reasoning, without being able to give any very explicit account of why this is so important.

v. Little questioning of the current programme of primary schools or 'middle-class values'.

vi. Minimal involvement in helping the parent to think about and solve her problems. (Such activities are felt to be a digression that is sometimes necessary in order to get the problem out of the way so that the 'real work' of the visit can go ahead.)

vii. Involving parents, in a class-room-like situation, in group activities designed to teach them the received wisdom about how to bring up their children.

Style 2

The home visitor who best exemplifies this approach takes the view that developmental learning follows interest. It is necessary to follow the child's interests and give him the information he needs to explore them. He will then come to observe and to think. He will pick up concepts in the process, and his need to observe and to think about his interests will lead him to develop these cognitive skills, which he will then use in order to master language. Thus, like Spearman (1927) and MacNamara (1972), she holds that the ability to perceive and think clearly is a prerequisite to the acquisition of language – not the reverse (cf Bereiter and Engelmann 1966).

Like Bruner (1966), Cazden (1974) and White (1976), her view is that the educator's job is to create environments in which children can grow. There is no need to direct their attention or to 'stamp in' basic constructs.

Like Kelly (1955), she holds that the child, like herself, is an experimenting, analysing, thoughtful being who is already trying to reflect on and improve the effectiveness of his actions, and trying to understand the world. Thus, it is not necessary to constrain his actions by rigid rules. Indeed, this is to be avoided so that the child can exercise these abilities.

In order to prevent the mother viewing the child as incompetent and ignorant (and therefore as something to be disciplined, trained, and instructed) but rather as competent, thoughtful, interested, and anxious to learn, she is eager to draw the mother's attention to her child's abilities and to encourage her to develop a respect for her child's competence.

Because the child is capable of reasoning, it is important to adopt discipline strategies that stress reason. But by reasoning with the child one also promotes the development of the ability to reason, question and analyse. The effect becomes cyclical.

In order to help the mother to become better able to model appropriate cognitive processes in action – for the child to see and copy – she encourages the mother to mull over the goals of the visiting, the success with which they are being achieved, and ways in which they could be attained more effectively.

In order to help them to think about children's behaviour, styles of interaction between parent and child, and educational processes, she encourages parents to visit the nursery school – where they can not only see teachers and children interacting, but also see parents interacting with their own and other children. They can also try out new styles of behaviour with other peoples' children in a situation in which the consequences of a mistake may be less serious than they would be with their own children.

Because of the subtlety of her approach to promoting growth and development she is doubtful about the notion that effective home-visiting could be carried out by mothers who have only a minimum of training and supervision.

Style 3

The third style of visiting is characterized by:

i.   A belief that it is necessary to use language to promote the development of reasoning ability.

ii. A belief that reasoning is impossible without language and concepts and that it is therefore necessary both to teach concepts and teach the analytic styles that are required to evolve concepts.

iii. A belief that an effort to help the mother to cope with her own problems will lead her to use language, get help from other people, make plans, anticipate the future, anticipate obstacles to the achievement of her goals and invent ways of surmounting them, bring to bear and utilize past experience, and increase her confidence in her ability to lead her life effectively. By doing these things more often in the child's presence, the mother will portray cognitive processes in action, and competent behaviour in general, in a way that it is easy for the child to copy. Indeed the child will have a strong inducement to copy it – because he will see that the behaviour helps the mother to achieve her goals effectively.

iv. A belief that helping the mother to deal with loneliness by reflecting on the nature of the problem and taking effective steps to deal with it in the way that has just been described is an activity that is *directly* relevant to the achievement of the main goals of the project – and not merely a means of getting one's foot in the door or a valuable side-effect of having been involved in the project.

v. A belief that schools urgently need to change away from their knowledge-communicating function to a growth-promotion function, but that, pending that change, children need to learn to take advantage of schools in exactly the same way as mothers need to learn how to exploit and manipulate bureaucracies in order to achieve their own ends.

Despite the attachment to language, this style veers toward the view of Bronfenbrenner that it is important to involve parents and children in activities in which the parents use cognitive activities to achieve their goals effectively. Although still some way from it, it also comes closest to the author's view that the language activities (so conspicuous to educational researchers in the past in the parent/child interactions of competent people) are only a small part of the total picture. So far as the child is concerned, the parental model also involves planning, monitoring the effects of one's behaviour and learning new things from the effects of that behaviour, and putting advancing oneself and the effective achievement of one's goals before attending to one's friends. These activities have an impact on development that is at least as important as the actual language activities that go on between a child and his mother.

Concluding Comment

Let us repeat. All of these are mixed strategies and the EHV who most closely exemplifies Style 3 claims to have begun as Style 2, been led by the literature to adopt a Style 1 approach and finally, as a result of what she learned as she went along, moved into a Style 3 position.

The Effects of the Project

Before discussing specific effects of the project mention should be made of one or two general effects, which may or may not always have been intended.

First, although some of the EHVs stress that they simply wish to give parents the option of changing their behaviour, they do not always recognize the power that role models have if these models are prestigeful, clear, and offer people a means of achieving some of their own most important goals. In this case that goal is to ensure that their children will be effortlessly successful in the school system and gain all the benefits which that success brings. The effects of a model are likely to be still more pronounced if, in addition to the characteristics that have already been mentioned, the values position espoused by the model is articulate, and culturally approved, while the alternative has not been made explicit, is contrary to the widely accepted wisdom of society and, if it exists, is held by people who have low status in society.

Also relevant to the EHVs' claim to be giving parents choice, is the fact that they are themselves unable to articulate any alternative values position which the parents they visit just might be adopting and which might explain their reluctance to take up some of the activities that the visitors would like them to adopt.

What possible meaning can be attributed to the notion of choice in the sort of context outlined?

In point of fact many of the parents seize on aspects of the EHV's behaviour that are clear, easily identifiable, imitable, and apparently directly relevant to the child's later success in the school system. Just as the general population has seized on education as the key that will give them access to the upper class's magic, so they seize on such things as reading *Ladybird* books instead of nursery rhymes to their children, on the importance of insisting that their children sit still, pay attention, and use materials in the way approved by the EHV, and set about using 'play' to teach language thereby, probably, destroying its general growth potential (an argument we do not have space to develop here).

But of the fact that the EHVs have an impact there is no doubt. The two questions are whether that impact is quite what they intended, and what the long-term consequences will be for the parent and child.

The next general theme on which we would like to comment is the role of loneliness. Many of the mothers are lonely and depressed. They welcome the visits as a means of alleviating their boredom. The regular visits give them something to look forward to, something to talk about to their children and their husband in between visits and a reason to keep their house tidy. They also have a sympathetic ear for their troubles. So far as can be judged this is one of the main reasons for welcoming the home visitors. (The other is their desire to find the magic needed to promote their children's success at school.)

In actual fact the visits do relieve loneliness and, as a result, family relationships improve. The parents become more relaxed and are likewise able to interact with their children in a more relaxed manner and pay more attention to them. Both the parents and their children flower and blossom. But two questions remain. First, was it the cognitively-oriented activity on the basis of which the project was justified to the Lothian Education Committee which promoted this development? And, secondly, has the child's *intellectual* capacity improved? Undoubtedly his school performance will improve if the mother's improved state of mental health bears up, because he will be less troubled by emotional problems and this is, of course, both an important outcome of the project and one that relates to the project's roots in *Born to Fail?* (Wedge and Prosser 1973) which showed that such children's school performance tends to be depressed relative to their IQ. But that is not directly related to the original cognitive emphasis of the project (though it is, indeed, directly relevant to trying to understand the nature of the problem the EHVs have been sent out to try to tackle).

The third general theme is associated with the last. Many of the mothers are isolated from grandparents and other mothers. They are therefore short of ideas on how to interest and amuse their children, and keep them out of mischief. When they see that their children look forward to the visits they become very positive indeed about them. Being able to keep one's children interested and out of mischief improves family relationships.

The parents become more inclined to acknowledge that, when their children complain or are disruptive, something is seriously wrong; they come to develop more *respect* for their children's views; they come to appreciate the abilities their children actually possess rather than focus on those they lack.

As a result of these changes in their perception of their children, it can be hypothesized that they will be more likely to 'want to know why' if their children do not do well at school – and be more likely to seek the reason in the environment rather than in the child himself. They will be more likely to accept the child's (rather than his teacher's) account of the reasons for his difficulties.

Once again this is an extremely important outcome of the project, and one that relates to its roots in *Born to Fail?* – but not one that seems to be directly related to the original, cognitive, theoretical formulation of the nature of the problem which was to be tackled and the guidance which was given to the EHVs.

A fourth comment to be made by way of general introduction is that, for many families, this is the child's first exposure to a pupil–teacher style of interaction. That mothers by mothering may be able to offer their children more and different things than teachers are able to offer them is not in dispute. But, whereas the middle-class parents include in their behavioural repertoire the tendency to, from time to time, adopt a teacherish style of behaviour when interacting with their children, this is not usually the case for the parents involved in this project. By teaching the child what to expect of a teacher and teaching him the culturally acceptable response to a teacher, the project may go a long way toward adjusting the child to school and thereby, once again, lessen his chance of becoming a problem and ensuring that his academic attainments are appropriate to his IQ.

The Impact on the Children's Cognitive Development

If we had tested the children's intelligence there is little doubt that it would have shown improvement.

Yet only one of the visitors, in relation to only two of the children she had visited, was confident that she had had a substantial impact on the children's cognitive development.

All the visitors found the task of trying to raise the child's cognitive functioning relative to other children of their age a great deal more difficult than they had anticipated.

That they had had other effects on the children's acceptance of others' adjustment, level of interest and so on is not denied. What we are concerned with here is the vexed question of whether cognitive development – which Peaker and Coleman, by not partialling out IQ in their regressions, have led many people to believe is largely determined by home process variables like talking to the child – is in fact affected in any significant way by such activities.

Most of the EHVs blamed their subjective feelings of disappointment with the results of their activities in this area on the perceived failure of the mothers to take up the activities they modelled. This subjective inability to achieve one of the central goals of the project is at least in part responsible for a feeling of being threatened by the evaluators which has become stronger over time. This feeling that, despite repeated assurances to the contrary, we were going to tell her (and everyone else) that her last two years' work had been a waste of time, was most pronounced in the EHV who stuck most closely to a Levenstein-type, cognitively-oriented, set of activities with the children and ventured least into family support activities or actions designed to promote the growth of the parents.

Now, what are we to make of this? Let us first focus on our assertion that had we tested the children's IQ the scores would have shown an increase. This assertion is based on the fact that activities undertaken by

1e EHVs with the children parallel those assessed in Merril-Palmer
:ales which are widely used to assess the effects of programmes of this
ort. In that test there are scales that assess the children's ability to cut
with scissors, match colours, fit shapes into holes, and use words. Since
1ese activities have been taught directly in the course of the visits,
1arked 'practice' effects would be expected. But the extent to which this
1crease would transfer to other tasks would remain doubtful. Further-
1ore, even if such skills did transfer to other abilities the desired increase
yould only be relevant to testing the 'critical period' type theory which
es behind the thinking of Levenstein and others if it were true that later
ognitive development is dependent on, rather than predictable from,
uccess in such early activities. To date we have not come across much
vidence to support this hypothesis.

What, then, are we to say about Bronfenbrenner's hypothesis – on
yhich the project was in part based – that cognitive 'gains' achieved
hrough early interventicn will be less likely to be 'lost' if the mother can
1e brought to interact with the child in a new way? (By way of context let
1s add that Levenstein (1978) has now dropped her claim that the gains
vill be less likely to be lost if the mother does take up these activities. The
eason why she has dropped this claim is also interesting: her controls –
vho had simply been told that they were taking part in an experiment –
ained as much as the experimental subjects.)

On logical grounds one would expect the children to lose their initial
.dvantage unless:

i. The parents moved on to other 'stimulating' activities, not
specified in this literature, but perhaps derivable from the work
of Douglas (1964), Peaker (1967, 1971, 1975) and Fraser
(1959), and, more plausibly, from the hypotheses advanced
by Bronfenbrenner in 1978 and those who advocate Style 3
intervention.

ii. Later cognitive development is dependent on mastery of these
early activities. If this is the case the mother's role is to ensure
that the child masters these activities early, rather than to
continue to interact with the child throughout his early development. If such critical period theory is correct, however, those who
wish to mount an intervention project will find themselves in a
double bind because they must assume that parents who have
not themselves mastered these necessary experiences early in life
can understand the subtle interactions that are required and
adopt them in adult life.

iii. The parents' expectations of the child and the child's self-image
have been markedly affected, in which case rather different

activities – such as feedback of normative data on the child
'brightness' to parent and child – might be indicated.

Our own hypothesis is that the EHVs are right. Although short-term
gains could be documented, little will remain in the long term unless the
project strategy changes in such a way as to prescribe activities for
parents (e.g. Style 3) that will enable parents to keep up the provision of
relevant cognitive stimulation. It seems to us that a precise experiment to
test Bronfenbrenner's (1974b) hypothesis, or Levenstein's theories – and
the associated critical period literature – would be negative. But clearly
as MacFadyen said in another paper, this is an issue of central
importance in the literature on which the project was based, and it is one
on which empirical evidence, as distinct from conjecture, is urgently
needed. We are therefore extremely anxious to extend the evaluation of
the project so that it will involve a detailed longitudinal (immediate and
long-term) analysis of subscore change and an opportunity to relate
subscore changes to the style adopted by the visitor.

Effects on the Children's Educational Development

It is clear that, by exposing the children to teacher-figures and a
teacherish/bookish style of adult/child interaction, the project will, as
Lazar (1977), Palmer (1977) and Love (1976) have shown in the United
States, have a marked impact on the children's acceptance of school. It
will reduce the chances of their being allocated to remedial classes and
designated as problem children. By avoiding these fates the children will
become less likely to be in school but not 'with' the class-room
curriculum. They will become better able to take advantage of the
educational opportunities that are open to them. Once again, obvious
though this appears to be, we must again repeat that, in our opinion, it is
essential to find out empirically whether this is true.

The hypothesis is that this effect will be greatest in Style 1 interaction.
Styles 2 and 3 may set up contradictory processes by leading the children
concerned to think for themselves and question the value of what is going
on at school. Indeed, the home visitors who have adopted these
approaches, but not those following a Style 1 interaction, share this
unease, although one of them also thinks that, in the long run, the effect
of pupils' questioning what goes on in schools will be to improve schools.

Style 2 may, however, promote the child's success in the school
system in another way. By leading the parent to realize that the child is
capable of making acute observations and able to reason, the EHV
may lead the parent to have an increased respect for the child's
capabilities, opinions and interests. Since parents generally expect

intelligent children to do well at school, the mother will be more likely to expect her child to do well there. If he does not she will be less likely to believe that the fault lies with the child and, as a result, more probably intervene actively with the school in order to promote the child's success. More than that, she may be more likely to take the child's opinions and complaints seriously and do something about them.

If we write 'educational development' with a small 'e', however, the balance sheet may be rather different. By focusing parents' and children's attention on the attainability of educational success, in the absence of activities that will effectively promote cognitive development, the growth of competence, initiative, system-awareness and self-confidence, the EHVs may be doing the children a disservice. As the author has shown elsewhere (Raven 1976), the well-known class variance in stress on independence, imagination, questioning, and intellectual behaviour, and its converse (stress on dependence, rule following and conforming behaviour) is anticipatory rather than either an effect of background or (as Kohn 1969 maintains) a result of experience in particular occupational roles. Thus, by focusing attention on the importance of school success, while at the same time failing to help children to develop the qualities needed to succeed in our society, the EHVs may prevent the parent and child focusing on the importance of the child developing toughness and strength, recognizing the importance of supporting friends who are in trouble and, instead, encourage the children to adopt a 'middle-class' value system (which stresses independence and personal competitive success). These expectations may well be frustrated. As the bench-mark data we discuss in a moment strongly suggests, it may be very important indeed for children who are going to live in a working-class environment to develop the abilities required to survive in a jungle-like world – and schools may not be the best places in which to foster these abilities. Intellectual activity may be required hardly at all in the jobs and life-styles the pupils are going to enter.

The train of thought set off by thinking about the probable impact of Styles 2 and 3 intervention also lead to another interesting question. The styles of interaction required to promote the development of independence of thought and behaviour, self-confidence, questioning scepticism, and the ability to learn without instruction may be extremely subtle. Those who wish to foster such qualities may therefore require a thorough understanding of the child's interests and need to be sensitive to the cues that indicate that the child could do with help to develop particular qualities. It may be important for the role models to whom he is exposed to portray effective behaviour in every aspect of their daily life.

Now, as the EHVs have observed, it is very difficult for someone who is not the child's mother to be sensitive to the meaning of slight gestures and intonations, to respond sensitively to the child or to model effective behaviour in a way that can be absorbed by the child. Mothering skills may be very different from, and a great deal more important than, teaching skills, and it may be extremely difficult for the EHVs to model them for parents. The objective of 'encouraging parents to recognize the importance of the crucial part that they play in promoting the educational development of their children' may have been corrupted to mean 'encouraging them to play a teacher's part and to get their children into nursery school as soon as possible'. If one recalls that the IEA data (1975) suggests that school systems that recruit children before 8 years of age confer few educational benefits on the children and that Tizard's (1974a) data suggests that schools are not very good at teaching children language, it emerges that the EHVs may, despite their professed objectives, be encouraging parents to *abdicate* their crucial role in promoting their children's development. They may well be contributing to our society's growing inability to make our children human.

Once again, these questions are of the greatest possible significance and they deserve to be followed up by further study of this project. So far the project has provided a unique opportunity to consider what is meant by growth and development, how that development is to be promoted, and to study parental attitudes and behaviour. Quite clearly it provides an excellent opportunity to study the effects of experimental attempts to influence patterns of mothering. But, equally clearly, the questions we are dealing with demand that we urgently develop the tools that will enable us to assess the effects of a project like this on the development of a broad spectrum of human competence – and not just on IQ and academic attainment.

Summary of Results from 'Illuminative' Work

In summary, lest there be any misunderstanding, let us repeat, first, that the project has had a major impact on our understanding of the nature of the problems that the project sought to address. If it has done nothing else, it has transformed the thinking of the teachers involved. That, in itself, is no mean achievement because those teachers will communicate their views to others. Secondly, it is abundantly clear that the mothers have adopted many of the activities modelled by the

EHVs, have become better able to amuse their children, have developed more respect for their children's abilities, have come to believe that they have a right to influence schools and are more likely to expect to be listened to, and have become more outgoing and more confident in their ability to lead their lives as they would like to lead them. All of these changes can be expected to have a significant impact on the subsequent development of their children. Thirdly, the project can be expected to have a major impact on the subsequent educational development of the children concerned, but through mechanisms that were not those which would be expected if one based one's model on a critical-period, early-cognitive-development theory.

However, despite these undoubted benefits, it is unlikely that the project will have a significant impact in stemming the 'drop off' effect which has been demonstrated for IQs in many intervention projects and which, it was hypothesized, would be countered by a project of this sort.

The Statistical Study

As we have already indicated, it proved possible to collect bench-mark data against which to view the home-visiting programme, and to assess the extent of the 'need' for it, from a substantial sample of parents living in the areas in which the home-visiting was taking place, and from an equally substantial sample of high socio-economic status parents.

These two samples are referred to as LSES and HSES respectively.

The sample sizes were, respectively, 200 and 80. For the reasons that were outlined earlier, it was possible to interview only forty-one mothers who had had home visits. Since the data were collected using two different interview schedules, the actual bases for many of the figures that will be given shortly are twenty and twenty-one individuals.

Despite these small sample sizes, many of the conclusions are based on observations from three independent sources: our own interviews and observations made in the course of the 'Illuminative' study, and each of the two interview schedules, which often collected parallel data using different techniques from each sample. Thus, small though the sample sizes are, the results we have obtained deserve to be taken seriously.

Figure 5.1 shows that, while the majority of HSES parents think it is very possible to influence the sort of person their child will grow up to be, only 20 per cent of the LSES group do so.

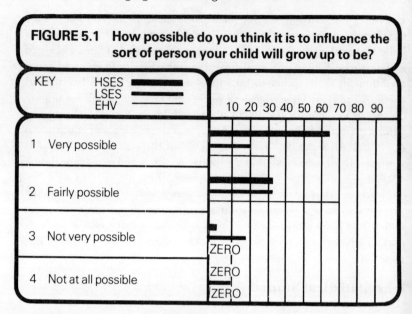

FIGURE 5.1   How possible do you think it is to influence the sort of person your child will grow up to be?

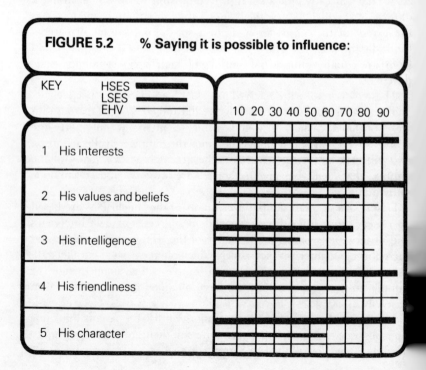

FIGURE 5.2   % Saying it is possible to influence:

Figure 5.2 shows that this difference is most marked in relation to intelligence and character, but it also affects all other characteristics.

Both figures also show that the home visitors have been able to have a major impact on this belief, particularly in relation to intelligence.

The data raise serious questions about who is right and, in particular, what is to be done to rescue those parents whose new-found faith turns out to be unfounded if the LSES parents are, indeed, correct in their view that it is not possible to have a substantial impact on such qualities.

It seems that both the background data and the data on the impact of the EHV programme make it essential to find out whether activities of the sort undertaken by the EHVs do in fact have a *major* impact on the development of character and intellect.

Given what we have seen of the styles adopted by the EHVs, it would seem that we owe our society a major responsibility to sort out the role of language in all this as a top priority.

Value for Intellectual Activity and the Perceived Importance of Language

Altogether we asked the parents to rate the importance they attached to sixty-seven possible goals in child-rearing, but the list was divided up so that no one person would be confronted by too long a list at any one point in time. The complete list is shown in Figure 5.9 on pages 125–130.

What is most striking about these results is the preoccupation of the HSES parents with intellectual activities and with fostering qualities, like independence, which are likely to be supportive of success in school and in HSES jobs.

The LSES group rates far fewer things 'very important', only three of their top thirteen priorities have to do with intellectual activity, and their top priorities have to do with their children having respect for them and needing them.

The EHVs have had a marked effect in consciousness raising, leading the parents they visited to rate many more things 'very important', and introducing an emphasis on an increased number of intellectual activities. Nevertheless, they have not changed the LSES stress on dependence rather than independence.

An examination of Figure 5.9 supports the notion that not only do HSES parents think it is much more important to involve their children in intellectual activities, they also seek to foster the child's intellectual growth and success in life *indirectly*, by fostering such qualities as independence, self-confidence, and the willingness to use books to find the information one wants.

Particular attention should be drawn to the last item. For LSES parents, there was sometimes active opposition to the child using books for his own purposes. As one parent said 'I wouldn't want that; you never know what he might come across poking about in books'. The desire to restrict opportunities to engage in original sin (curiosity) could not be more apparent.

This is one indication among many that the HSES preoccupation with language and intellectual activities – on which many psychologists have tended to focus in the past – is only part of a wider constellation of interrelated attitudes that involve such things as discipline strategies, 'respect', and fostering independence, initiative, adventurousness, and an inquiring mind.

The data strongly suggest that it is a grave mistake to focus on intellectual and language activities without this wider context, and the degree to which the EHVs have found themselves drawn into activities related to this wider context, despite injunctions to the contrary, strongly supports this contention.

Attention may also be drawn to the difficulty that HSES researchers have in finding items that LSES informants will rate 'very important'. Even when one has found them, as in the item 'that your children really need you', one starts to ask oneself what such a view may mean in a way which serves to invalidate the very item that so many people have endorsed.

The significance of this observation is this: if, as the author has argued elsewhere (Raven 1977), people will only behave in a competent manner, i.e. use language to bring to bear relevant past experiences, anticipate obstacles to achieving their goals, strive to think of ways round those obstacles, and so on, in relation to goals they value, then it is quite inappropriate to seek to find out whether people are *able* to engage in these complex and demanding activities in relation to goals they do not value.

Our data strongly suggest that, had we studied our informants' ability and willingness to talk about their goals, make explicit ways of achieving them, reflect on the causes of previous successes and failures etc., in relation to such goals as ensuring their children were dependent on them, had 'respect' for them, were strong and tough, and were able to stick up for themselves, we would indeed have found that they were behaving in ways that indicated an understanding of competent behaviour which was every bit as complete as that evinced by HSES parents in relation to intellectual goals.

Further support for this proposition will be found in the discussion that follows.

Impact of EHVs

Despite all these reservations, the home visitors appear to have had a major impact on the parents' beliefs across a wide variety of outcomes. It is more important for their child to spend a lot of time with his parents, to talk to his parents about what he is doing, to have books in the home, to have educational toys, to question and seek reasons for things he is told, to play with sand and water, to develop inventiveness, inquisitiveness and interests and tastes that are different from those of others, and to do well at school.

The parents have come to believe that they themselves should read to their children, ask them questions about books and things they have seen, teach them to think for themselves, talk to them a lot, encourage them to ask questions, continue the work of the school in the home, help them to think clearly about what they are trying to do, and take them to public libraries.

Nevertheless, in some respects, they have led the home-visited group to move away from the HSES group. This applies particularly to school activities like studying on their own, continuing the work of the school in the home and the child doing well at school.

There seems to be more pressure for school success, rather than a tendency to foster qualities that are likely to make for school and life success indirectly by fostering independence, initiative, confidence in dealing with new people and new situations, and the ability to think for oneself.

There has been no change in the proportion who thought it was important for the child to use books to find information for himself, to learn to settle down and concentrate, to his feeling confident with people and situations he has not met before, or to providing affective rewards for achievement. There was relatively little impact on the parents thinking it was important to treat their children with respect, as individuals in their own right who were entitled to interests and ideas of their own.

Autonomous Learning and Language Learning

The absence of change of these items, which may well be crucial to the development of autonomous learning – the ability to make one's own observations and learn without instruction – is striking. Without a spontaneous tendency to make one's own observations and learn without instruction, one may fail to develop the basic abilities that are required to discern and acquire language competence. More than this, if one is not treated with respect, as an individual entitled to one's own views and opinions, one is unlikely to come to think of oneself as the sort of person who is capable of having one's own views and opinions, one is unlikely to reason and to seek to persuade others of the quality of one's reasoning – because one will learn that such activities do not in fact move one toward one's goals.

Effects on Parents

Not only may parents' unwillingness to respect and have confidence in their children result in the child not developing a spontaneous tendency to rely on such abilities, it may also deprive the parent of evidence that the child is capable of reasoning. If the parents are deprived of this information, they may be more likely to be prescriptive and directive in their language and commands to the child. If a child brought up in this way draws his parents' attention to environmental barriers to his learning when he gets to school, his parents may well be more likely to dismiss his complaints and blame *him* rather than the environment, because they will not already have learned that he is capable of making acute observations and reasoning about the sources of his problems.

Thus, differential language activities in the home may be a product of a much wider set of values and environmental constraints and may not bear a causal relationship to school life and success.

The home visitors, by encouraging parents to see a direct link between school and life success, and language and school success, may be leading the parents to have expectations that will not be fulfilled.

Talking to children may well not promote school success, and school success, in the absence of the much wider qualities that HSES parents seek to foster, may not make for life success.

Not only may differential language activity be a product of wider attitudes, these wider attitudes may be more important determinants of life success than the conspicuous difference in language. The HSES mothers much more often than LSES mothers expect their children to be able to concentrate, act responsibly, and reason. They therefore regard their children as possessing most of the abilities and motivations possessed by adults. As a result of expecting them to possess these abilities they may well be more likely to lead their children to exercise them. Under these circumstances they may be less likely to feel obliged to coerce their children into 'desirable' activities and be less directive and prescriptive – because the children are already thought to be capable of recognizing the danger of particular situations and doing what it is best to do to achieve their long-term goals. As a result of having developed internalized, goal-oriented controls over their own behaviour the children may be able to adventure and be inquisitive without encountering danger. Independence, initiative, inquisitiveness, adventurousness, and confidence in one's own abilities and in other people's willingness to respond to one's reasoning and requests, may make for a life-style that pays a wide variety of dividends. The ability to concentrate, the willingness to observe and think for oneself, the willingness and ability to reason with others and expect them to change their point of view, the tendency to study causal sequences, the ability to find information one needs in books, and the ability to lead others to recognize the value of one's contribution, may all represent a context for language activity that is of more importance than language itself. Home visitors may find themselves hard put to influence such a wide range of beliefs and attitudes.

Are HSES Parents' Beliefs about the Efficacy of Child-Rearing Processes Correct?

Although the possible consequences of different discipline strategies and the fostering of qualities like originality, independence and thinking for oneself seem fairly obvious, it is necessary to question whether these patterns of socialization actually have the effects that would be expected.

In an earlier study (Raven 1976) the author has shown that downwardly mobile children, who come from backgrounds in which independence, originality, and intellectual activities are stressed, are more likely than others from their backgrounds to stress the need for firm, prescriptive rules and discipline, and they are less likely to value independence, originality, and thinking for oneself. The HSES differences in attitudes and behaviour reported above may therefore be a product of differential attitudes and abilities and these differences may not have the effects on their children that one would expect. Rather, the differences in the attitudes and behaviour of children who come from different backgrounds may be a result of other, as yet poorly understood, processes. Because of basic constitutional differences it may be just too difficult for children bound for low socio-economic status positions in society to engage in the complex reasoning processes that underlie internalized controls of behaviour. Independence, and thinking for oneself may be just too difficult for them. In other words, LSES parents may be LSES parents precisely because they lack the ability to think through these issues. Alternatively, it may be that downwardly mobile pupils can see that they are unlikely to require intellectual activity, and self-motivated behaviour, in the types of jobs they are going to enter.

Either way, LSES parents are likely to be much less practised in the sort of activities that are required to cope easily with independent children. Indeed their stress on their children needing them may be a product of their need to retain control over them in a straightforward manner, because any other form of control may simply be too difficult for them.

Implications of the Variance in Values

There is one further aspect of Figure 5.9 to be considered in passing. This is that it is clear that no amount of Educational Home Visiting will get rid of the variance in parents' objectives in child-rearing. As we have seen, that variance is pretty fundamental and must have some functional significance. It seems that many of the goals we have discussed are quite incompatible in a single school class-room. One cannot, at the same time, encourage some children to question authority and others to be instantly obedient to it. One cannot encourage some children to be original and creative, and others to learn what is put in front of them. One cannot encourage some children to be sensitive to the fleeting feelings that lie at the heart of literary, artistic and scientific creativity and seek to repress curiosity in others. Although it would be possible to cater for some of this variance by individualizing educational provision, we will see that most parents are opposed to this. It therefore seems that one of the critical tasks that the home visitors need to carry out is to bring parents to understand and accept those types of educational provision that would make it possible to cater for this variation in felt needs. Unless this is done, *nobody's* needs will be satisfied, least of all the felt needs of those who are most concerned with independence, initiative, the ability to observe and learn without instruction, and sensitivity to those fleeting feelings of a fringe of consciousness which tell one that one has the germ of a creative idea. In other words it may be of critical importance for home visitors to make explicit, and to share with parents, the nature of the alternative goals that could be pursued by parents and teachers, and the ways in which those goals might be achieved.

In other words, the central role of language in home-visiting might be to give parents the concepts that they need to think about the nature of human talent, the ways in which it is to be fostered, and the institutions of their society.

Why Are Certain Activities Believed to Be Important or Unimportant?

We asked mothers why they thought some of the activities were important. Our results indicate their reasons for thinking it is important to ask their children questions. For the HSES group the most common reason was to encourage the child to understand, find out and take an interest in things. For the LSES group it was to teach the child to recognize things and learn their names.

This difference in emphasis seems to reflect a difference between an emphasis on cognitive *processes* – understanding, observing, and reasoning – and an emphasis on cognitive *knowledge*. In this context we may suggest that Bereiter and Englemann (1966) may simply be reinforcing LSES parents' feelings that it is important to ask children questions in order to teach them knowledge.

LSES parents were also more likely than HSES parents to think it was important to ask children 'tutorial' questions to see whether they were learning and what they were learning. This emphasis on 'testing' the child reflects a feeling that the child would not learn spontaneously if he was not prodded in this way, and this might be construed as further evidence that LSES parents tend to distrust their children's motivation and competence. Of course, the children they are dealing with may actually *be* less competent and motivated and therefore need more prodding.

The home visitors have reduced the frequency with which LSES parents said that asking children questions was a means of encouraging them to recognize things around them. They have led them to place still more emphasis on questioning the child after the manner of a teacher.

When parents were asked why it was important to look at books with a child, the HSES group were more likely to say that it developed language, imagination, creativity and concentration.

The EHVs have been extraordinarily successful in leading the parents they visited to think that such activities are valuable because they are interesting and enjoyable. They have been much less successful in leading them to think that such activity might be responsible for the growth of other competencies just mentioned.

The results show that the main impact of the home visitors has been to virtually double both the proportion who thought it was important to read to the child in order to please him and the proportion who thought that it would promote the development of the child's language. Perhaps the reason why parents more often associate reading stories to their children, rather than just talking to them, with the development of language is that stories in books are more likely to contain more sophisticated words and, in particular, to be expressed in 'correct' forms of speech.

We have already seen that HSES parents were more likely than LSES parents to think that it was very important to talk to their children a lot.

More HSES than LSES parents thought that lack of conversation between parent and child would cause poor language development, feelings of rejection, poor intellectual development, poor progress at school, boredom and unhappiness, and failure of parent and child to get to know each other. The data shows how very important communication is to most HSES parents. HSES parents are obviously much more inclined to see it as a means of getting to know their children – and this may be of particular importance if they wish to facilitate the child's growth by enabling him to pursue his own interests.

The view that it is not really important to talk to their children was often expressed by LSES mothers.

'It wouldn't really matter. If I never spoke to him he'd pick it up outside anyway, or at the school. He'd learn somehow.'

It is quite clear that the home visitors cannot expect the parents they visit to share many of their own assumptions about the importance of communication between parent and child. However, the accuracy of those assumptions, while most logical, is open to question.

While most parents associated question-asking with the development of a tendency to work things out for oneself, developing one's own opinions, independence and responsibility, the HSES group was more likely to do all of these things. They were also more likely to associate question-asking with the development of language.

It would also appear, from data not presented here, that it is not true that LSES parents do not see the connection between encouraging children to ask questions and seek reasons for things they are told and cognitive and character development. They see the connection but they do not particularly value the qualities that they expect children to develop if they encourage them to ask questions.

What is more, less than half of either group thought that questioning, reasoning people would be more likely to get on at school or in life – which perhaps indicates that HSES parents value these qualities for their intrinsic rather than their instrumental benefits. One of the effects of the home-visiting has in fact been to lead the mothers to think that the child who questions and seeks reasons for things he has been told will be more likely to do well at school.

Most parents from both groups anticipated that treating the child as an individual who was entitled to pursue his own interests and ideas would lead him to have opinions of his own, to be able to work things out for himself and to be independent and responsible. Once again, therefore, it would seem that failure to think the activity important is not a product of not understanding the consequences of not doing it, but rather a result of a differing evaluation of those consequences.

One thing that emerges from these results is, therefore, that it would be a mistake to imagine that the home-visited parents' tendency to think that some of the activities which were rated 'very important' have come about for the reasons we would tend to assume. In the case of at least some of the sub-group of items we have studied in detail, the reasons that lay behind the home-visited parents' responses were unexpected, and in some ways foreign to us.

From the data we have presented it seems likely that parents desperately want to enjoy their relationship with their children, and have seized upon many of the activities encouraged by the home visitors as potential ways of helping them to enjoy that relationship. Unfortunately, as we shall see later, either because they are not able to engage in these activities more frequently, or for some other reason, they do not actually seem to enjoy their relationship with their children any more. Data from informal interviews suggests that the reason for this is that although they find that they do indeed come to enjoy the activities that the EHVs demonstrate, and discover that their children enjoy them a great deal more than they thought, they just do not have the time to spend with their children in these activities. They seem to be too preoccupied with gaining a precarious hold on life. There are recurrent indications (though admittedly no clear proof) that this is so; it emerges when they are asked about the quality of their lives, the problems they expect their children to encounter as they get older, and the ways in which they could help their children to do better at school. By giving the mothers a taste for something that they cannot obtain, the home visitors may, therefore, have led them to feel increasingly frustrated, although this is a hypothesis that we cannot test from the present data.

Nevertheless, if family relationships do improve that might indeed give the children a greater opportunity to flower and develop. The parents may come to realize how competent they are and, as a result, come to rely on them more and stretch them more and, by taking their children's complaints seriously and doing something about them, they may reinforce their children's tendency to make logical requests and express them in a reasoned and linguistically coherent form. What are being observed in the home-visited parents' responses may be a gut reaction to the effect that the *first* priority is to improve family relationships – without any clear understanding of why it is so important to improve those relationships or what would follow from so doing. If it is the case that this is what is happening, and if improving family relationships is a more important way of promoting cognitive development than promoting early intellectual activity, then the implications for the design of home-visiting programmes and the priorities of the home visitors could be considerable. However, even if this is the correct way to construe the problem, it is, as the EHVs have observed, often easier to gain an entrée to the home situation by focusing on the children, their play and their education, than by focusing directly on the interpersonal inadequacies of the parents.

How Can Growth Be Facilitated?

In addition to asking parents what the consequences would be if they did, or did not, do various things with their children, we asked them what they thought they could do to develop three of the qualities that they themselves had said were very important.

Figure 5.3 shows that there were substantial differences between the groups in what they thought they might do to help their children to develop their intelligence.

The majority of HSES parents said that a parent could help a child to develop his intelligence by talking to him, discussing things with him and answering his questions. Less than half the LSES parents who thought that intelligence was important gave answers that fell into this category. Likewise, 69 per cent of the HSES group thought that intelligence could be fostered by giving a child plenty of attention, taking an interest in him and playing with him, compared with only 16 per cent of the LSES group. The responsiveness of HSES parents *to* a child could not be more apparent.

The next most frequently mentioned category for the HSES group was providing and encouraging the use of books (HSES 39 per cent; LSES 13 per cent). The answers that were grouped into this category make it quite clear that HSES parents give their children tremendous encouragement when they are doing things and using information instead of being a passive recipient of information.

These results support the suggestion that many parents in LSES areas seem to equate 'intelligence' with 'the ability to do school work' and often do not think that being intelligent involves more than doing reading, writing, and arithmetic. They focus on the knowledge of content and specific skills, rather than process.

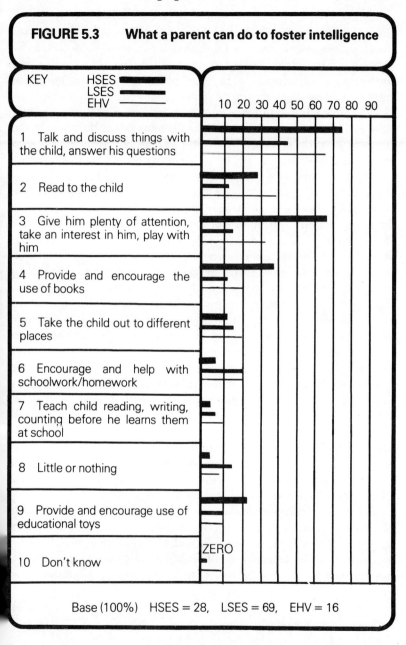

FIGURE 5.3   What a parent can do to foster intelligence

KEY   HSES ▬▬▬
       LSES ▬▬▬
       EHV ————

10 20 30 40 50 60 70 80 90

1   Talk and discuss things with the child, answer his questions

2   Read to the child

3   Give him plenty of attention, take an interest in him, play with him

4   Provide and encourage the use of books

5   Take the child out to different places

6   Encourage and help with schoolwork/homework

7   Teach child reading, writing, counting before he learns them at school

8   Little or nothing

9   Provide and encourage use of educational toys

ZERO

10   Don't know

Base (100%)   HSES = 28,   LSES = 69,   EHV = 16

Figure 5.3 also shows that home visitors have led significant proportions of those parents who thought it was important for their children to
develop their intelligence to think that the parent could do this by
reading to the child, talking to him, discussing things with him,
answering his questions, giving him plenty of attention, taking an
interest in him, and playing with him. They have actually led the
home-visited sample to place more emphasis on reading to the child
than the HSES group and have almost eliminated the difference in the
frequency with which the HSES and LSES groups mention talking to
the child and discussing things with him. However, they have by no
means eliminated the enormous difference between the proportions of
the HSES and LSES groups who thought that intelligence was to be
fostered by giving the child plenty of attention, taking an interest in
him, and playing with him. Nor have they substantially reduced the
difference between the two groups in the proportion who thought it was
important to provide and encourage the child to use books for himself.
We will see later that HSES parents were much more likely than
LSES parents to say that most of the child's activities were joint
activities in which both parent and child participated. In that context,
it may be conjectured that, not only are the HSES parents much more
inclined to stress pro-active rather than reactive behaviour on the part
of the child, they are also much more likely to be sensitively responsive
to the child's needs. Whereas the LSES group seem to make a sharp
distinction between activities the child initiates – which encompass
most of his activities – and their own teaching (i.e. telling) activities,
the HSES group seem to be more facilitative of development, and
sensitively responsive to child-initiated activities. The home visitors
seem to have had little success in leading the parents they visited to
adopt such a transactional viewpoint. Once again this is a conjecture
that seems to be emerging from the data, rather than a finding that has
been fully substantiated within the present inquiry.

Figure 5.4 is important because it shows that HSES and LSES
parents propose to foster respect in totally different ways. The LSES
group proposes to insist upon it, and to insist upon unquestioning
obedience, while the HSES group feels that they have to earn respect.
One group thinks that respect is to be fostered by being firm and
maintaining discipline, the other by talking to the child about one's
reasons for one's actions, and by respecting the child. One group feels it
is to be fostered by doing things *to* the child, and the other feels it is to
be fostered by setting a good example.

These differences highlight findings that pervade our work. The
HSES group teach by reasoning, by example, and by responding to the

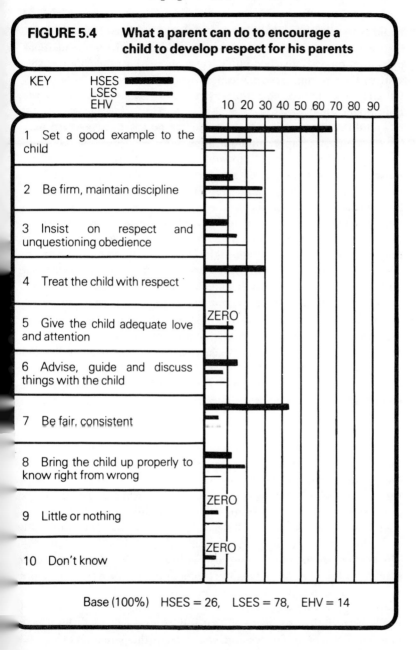

FIGURE 5.4   What a parent can do to encourage a child to develop respect for his parents

KEY   HSES
       LSES
       EHV

10 20 30 40 50 60 70 80 90

1 Set a good example to the child

2 Be firm, maintain discipline

3 Insist on respect and unquestioning obedience

4 Treat the child with respect

5 Give the child adequate love and attention   ZERO

6 Advise, guide and discuss things with the child

7 Be fair, consistent

8 Bring the child up properly to know right from wrong

9 Little or nothing   ZERO

10 Don't know   ZERO

Base (100%)   HSES = 26,   LSES = 78,   EHV = 14

child. The LSES group teach in a schoolmasterly fashion. Nothing could better illustrate the dilemma for the Educational Home Visitors. As we have indicated, by introducing children to the preoccupations and questioning of teachers, they will help to adjust the children they visit to the working-class institutions which schools seem to be. They will help them to succeed in those systems. But is that what really needs to be done?

The differences in the way in which respect is to be fostered may have a number of important implications.

A parent who is concerned to *earn* respect will obviously try to behave in ways that are deserving of respect. He or she will therefore be inclined to behave in a way that is above reproach, will be more likely to discuss his or her actions, the reasons for them, and their long-term consequences with the child. These considerations may involve the future of the child, his family, or the society in which the family lives. To do these things the parent not only has to talk to the child, but also to make his or her own values clear, to share his or her understanding of human behaviour and the workings of the family and society with the child, and to share his or her understanding of cause and effect in human behaviour.

If parental behaviour is to be seen by the child as fair and considerate the parent must engage the child in a similarly complex set of cognitive activities. And the parent must make clear value-dilemmas, the ways in which they can be resolved, the sorts of information that it is appropriate to bring to bear to resolve them, the sorts of behaviours they themselves value and their reasons for valuing them, and the barriers to living up to their ideals and the ways in which, by taking thought, those barriers can be crossed.

An effort to treat the child with respect is likely to create opportunities for the child to talk, to reason (with authority), to consider the long-term consequences of his actions, and to make explicit and discuss the values, codes, and long-term considerations which should guide his actions. Not only will these activities lead the child to practice complex cognitive activities, they will lead him to imagine and anticipate possible long-term consequences of his actions with which he may not already be familiar, to imagine barriers to his achieving his goals, to consider a broad range of possibly conflicting consequences and choose between them, to develop confidence in his ability to handle such ideas, to think of himself as someone who is capable of handling such ideas, to think of authority as something that is open to reason and which he is entitled to seek to influence and, above all, if the parent *does* treat the child with respect and respond to his arguments, to experience the benefits of sound rational argument.

In the course of the sorts of discussions that are implied in such a pattern of interaction between parent and child, the child will obviously be exposed to an extremely wide range of viewpoints and ideas. As a result, he is likely to find further new ideas a great deal less unfamiliar and frightening. He will have more pegs on which to hang them. He will therefore be more open to new ideas and innovations and more likely to explore their relevance to his own behaviour.

The development of a spontaneous tendency to guide one's own behaviour by reference to the probable long-term consequences of one's actions for oneself, one's family and one's society should also lead to the development of internalized controls. Such flexible internalized controls should result in curiosity, initiative and adventurousness being a great deal less dangerous. It may also lead the parent to realize just how competent their children are, how logical and valid are their reasons for their actions, and to discover their children's interests and motivations. Parents may also come to adapt the children's environment so that it becomes possible for the children to pursue their interests and thereby develop the other components of competence to which we have referred.

In short, as the EHVs, Brandis and Bernstein (1974), Hess and Shipman (1965) and others, have recognized, the mutual respect and discipline issue is central to cognitive development. Yet it poses serious value-laden problems for those who wish to implement projects such as that being evaluated here.

Yet, despite the apparent logic of this position, that logic may well be wrong. Quite obviously any parent who is to behave like the HSES parents must be extremely competent at cognitive activity themselves. And it may well be that many LSES parents have moved into LSES jobs and come to seek prescriptive moral codes to guide their behaviour precisely *because* they are less able to reason and cope with complex arguments. This hypothesis finds some support in the data (Raven 1976), where we found that downwardly mobile pupils, who had presumably been exposed to the HSES child-rearing practices described here, were more likely to wish to have prescriptive codes laid down for them and were more anxious that they be firmly enforced than were other children from similar backgrounds.

The conclusions to which this data and discussion seem to be leading us are, therefore:

i.   That children from different backgrounds are likely to have been exposed to different patterns of discipline and to expect different patterns of discipline from teachers and other authorities.

ii. That different *parents* are likely to expect teachers and

ii.   authorities to exercise authority in different ways because they
        focus on different consequences of those patterns of authority.

iii.   That children from different backgrounds are likely to value
        and respect different patterns of behaviour in teachers and
        authority.

iv.   That the different attitudes we are dealing with here may be
        either the cause, or the effect, of variations in levels of intellectual
        activity and moral reasoning.

What are the implications of these results for Educational Home-
visiting programmes and Educational Home Visitors?

One clear implication is that cognitive activity is not an isolated
activity, but something that is inextricably bound up with other values,
perceptions and expectations. To intervene effectively in one area of
this system of beliefs and expectations it may be necessary to have an
understanding of the whole. Conversely, an intervention in one part of
the system may well have unexpected repercussions on other attitudes,
beliefs and behaviours. There is a clear need to make more of the
system explicit. One way of doing this is to intervene in a variety of
different ways and to monitor the effects of so doing over a wide range
of potential outcomes – including apparently unconnected consequences for the parents, their children, and the schools the children
attend.

An Educational Home Visitor who encourages the parents she visits
to reason with their children may set up acute conflicts. The parent
may be *unable* to reason, and may not *value* the questioning, inquiring,
self-reliant activity that may follow. On the other hand the EHV may
be right: by encouraging parents to reason with their children she may
not only stimulate the development of the child's reasoning abilities,
but also lead the mother to be less dismissive of the child's abilities and
opinions and, in the long run, therefore be more willing to intervene on
the child's behalf if all is not going well for him at school.

Parents as Teachers

Our results further enable us to develop our theme that the cognitive
and language activities which differentiate HSES and LSES parents
are only part of a wider picture which encompasses, but does not
consist of, the language and cognitive activities with which previous
researchers have so often been preoccupied. HSES parents, while being
more inclined than LSES parents to say that their children learn a lot
from them, actually say that they set out to teach them less and that the
child learns more himself. In their view, parents facilitate the develop-

ment of their children by setting an example and by responding in a sensitive manner to the child's activities. EHVs therefore appear to have a serious dilemma if they wish to encourage the parents they visit to behave like HSES parents – because these parents behave in ways that are different from those which teachers tend to employ in class-rooms. The problem of inadequate mothering – which the home-visiting programme set out to tackle – would seem to have much more to do with encouraging the mothers to focus on *facilitating the development of*, rather than *teaching*, their children.

When LSES parents set out to teach their children, they are not inclined to teach intellectual skills. The home visitors appeared to have had a dramatic effect on this. They had had less effect in reducing the discrepancy between HSES and LSES parents' emphasis on teaching independence and physical skills.

There is a dramatic difference between the HSES and LSES groups on how they teach their children these things. The majority (67 per cent) of HSES parents teach by setting an example, followed by 36 per cent who teach by giving reasons and explanations and 28 per cent who teach by providing a stimulating environment.

The LSES most often teach by giving constant reminders – i.e. by nagging, setting an example (but only 23 per cent said this), and punishing failure (22 per cent) (which usually means smacking).

The home visitors appear to have had much less effect on how parents teach their children than on what they teach them.

Asking Questions

As we have seen, there was a big difference between the proportion of HSES and LSES parents who thought that it was important to encourage their children to ask questions (60 per cent compared with 37 per cent). The HSES parents were more confident that they would be able to answer their children's questions and, although more than half of them did sometimes find them a nuisance, they were less likely to do so than the LSES parents.

As the Newsons (1968, 1978) and Bernstein (1971) have also found, LSES parents were more likely to make up answers when they did not know the answer. They were less likely to look up the answer in books. This may be because they did not have books readily available, or it may be because they had not themselves come to use books as a source of information.

The home-visited parents' answers to these questions differed hardly at all from those of the LSES group – a fact that may indicate that the

EHVs had only the slightest impact on some attitudes which are fundamental to the child's appreciation of the role of books and intellectual inquiry.

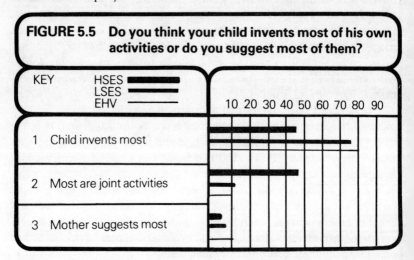

FIGURE 5.5   Do you think your child invents most of his own activities or do you suggest most of them?

Figure 5.5 reveals a dramatic difference between the proportions of HSES and LSES parents who say that while the child initiates most activities, they end up by being joint activities. The EHVs do not appear to have had any effect on this. The HSES parents seem to be able to strike a seemingly sensitive balance between responding to the child, capitalizing on teaching situations, emphasizing cognitive development, and facilitating the growth of other competencies. Their way of proceeding is most *unlike* the balance that one tends to observe in class-rooms – or even on home visits. To strike that balance it may be necessary to have a great deal of time and to be sensitive to the child's interests. The most important thing EHVs have to teach parents may not be *what* to do with their children, but how to create growth-enhancing environments and how to *respond* sensitively to child-initiated activities (White 1976).

What Do Parents Talk about to Their Children?

Figure 5.6 shows what parents said they talked about to their children while they were engaged in some joint educational activity such as doing jigsaws or making things in the kitchen.

The most common type of dialogue between LSES mothers and their children takes the form of warnings and instructions from the mother to the child.

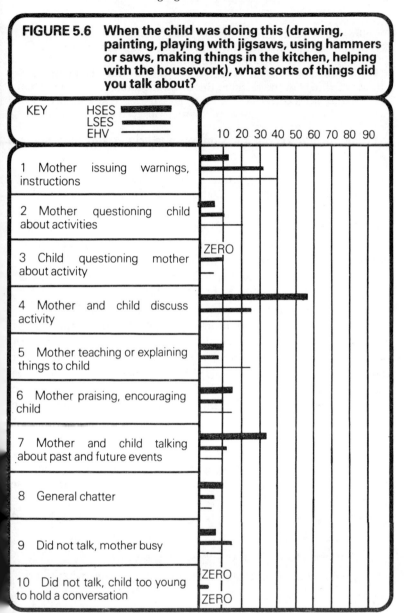

FIGURE 5.6 **When the child was doing this (drawing, painting, playing with jigsaws, using hammers or saws, making things in the kitchen, helping with the housework), what sorts of things did you talk about?**

KEY   HSES ▬▬▬
       LSES ━━━
       EHV ─────

10 20 30 40 50 60 70 80 90

1 Mother issuing warnings, instructions

2 Mother questioning child about activities

3 Child questioning mother about activity   ZERO

4 Mother and child discuss activity

5 Mother teaching or explaining things to child

6 Mother praising, encouraging child

7 Mother and child talking about past and future events

8 General chatter

9 Did not talk, mother busy

10 Did not talk, child too young to hold a conversation   ZERO   ZERO

'Get lost!'.
'Telling him to hurry up – and what was coming on TV next'.
'What do you think you're doing? You're giving mum more work'.
'Can't remember. Probably "Clear off"'.
'To put legs and eyes on the people he was drawing. To be careful –
to watch things in the kitchen: the stove, the knife. . . . Showing him
how to do things correctly'.
'Telling him to cut down the noise, do it quickly' (child was
drawing).
'Telling them to get out and stop trying to help. Asking them to tidy
up their room'.
'Mainly giving her a row for doing things she's not allowed'.
'Not to get herself soaking. Not to break the dishes'.
'What to do next. What to do and what not to do'.
'To make less noise'.

While HSES mothers also issued warnings and instructions these
came in fourth place behind other sorts of conversation. Most common
for them was discussion of the activities that were being undertaken.

'Talking about weighing out flour, putting in water, mixing and
stirring. Dusting, cleaning, scrubbing, polishing!'

The second most common topic for HSES parents and children was
the discussion of past and future events, followed by the mother
praising and encouraging the child.

Both groups of mothers were equally likely to question the child
about what he was doing but no HSES parent mentioned that the child
questioned her, while 9 per cent of LSES parents did so. This could
possibly indicate that HSES mothers volunteer more information
without having to be asked.

The mother teaching or explaining things to the child was not very
common.

LSES mothers were more likely than HSES mothers to say they did
not talk at all because mother was too busy or working elsewhere in the
house:

'Nothing. It's the only time I get any peace. I let him do it himself'
(child drawing).

LSES parents tended to give very specific directions:

'Just telling him what to do, where to dust and wipe, what to bring
me, and not to go round pulling everything out as soon as I'd cleared
it'.

The HSES were much more open and responsive, and demanded
more independence, initiative and responsibility from the child:

'I asked her how she was going to begin; she told me, and then she
got on and did it'.

Bernstein (1971), Tough (1973), Hess and Shipman (1965) and others have also drawn attention to such differences in the quality of language in the homes of children who come from different backgrounds.

At the very least, these two patterns of interaction would be expected to lead the children to develop different expectations of, and attitudes towards, the use of language. The LSES pattern of interactions seems likely to lead the child to expect that, if someone speaks to him in the context of such activities, it will be to issue specific directions, commands and warnings – and he may well come to depend on such close supervision if he is to undertake such tasks. That the child should be dependent on his mother in this way is, of course, just what the mother intended. An alternative explanation of the difference is, however, that the parents' behaviour is dependent on the fact that their children are, in general, less likely to be able to carry out such tasks satisfactorily without constant supervision and direction.

Before we obtained the data from home-visited samples we noted that encouraging parents to talk to their children might result only in an increase in such specific, directive behaviour – and this is indeed just what we have observed. There is therefore a clear case for encouraging the EHVs to consider more carefully the *type* of language interaction they encourage.

The case for doing this becomes stronger the more one reflects on the implications of the differences between the two groups. The biggest differences are in connection with the amount of discussion of activity with the child and conversations about what is happening, has happened, or will happen.

Conversations about what is happening, in addition to conveying knowledge, may give the child a great deal of insight into cognitive processes in action. The parent may share with the child her understanding of what is going on, her tendency to try to understand cause and effect, her tendency to think about what is likely to happen, her plans and her initiatives designed to take corrective action to achieve her goals, her tendency to monitor what happens and intervene appropriately if necessary, her rejection, or modification, of certain strategies if it becomes clear that they are going to encounter obstacles, and her feelings about the activity itself and the goals she hopes to achieve. In short, she may model for the child the components of competence and the springs of motivation in action. She imagines, she dredges in her mind for relevant past experiences, and she anticipates the future. Her feelings, the past and the future, her plans and her knowledge are finely balanced determinants of present activity, and not separated from it. The whole process is most *un*like the formal separation of intellectual activity from action which is so clearly apparent in schools and in the thinking of many LSES parents. And all this is done in the context of encouraging the child to join in in his own way. How should the EHVs model for parents this integrated and finely balanced pattern of activity?

In the context of such reflections it may be suggested that the observed increase in the frequency with which mothers reported questioning their child about their activities is reminiscent of the pedagogue's tendency to question a child in order to *test* him – to find out if he already knows something they already know, rather than to learn from the child, and it will be recalled that this seemed to be one of the effects of the home visitors on the things parents thought it was important to do with their children.

One should, however, be wary of generalizing too far on the basis of our data. Our questions asked LSES parents what they talked about in the course of activities which they did not, in all honesty, believe to be of the greatest importance (although they *are* the activities that the EHVs try to encourage them to undertake with their children). As we have seen, they were more likely to think it was important for them to ensure that their children were *dependent* on them and learnt to stick up for themselves. As we have commented, their behaviour seems ideally suited to the achievement of the first goal. And we have also seen that at least some LSES parents do go to some considerable lengths to *show* their children how to fight – and it may well be that, had we asked what they talked about while they were doing so, we would have found that they discussed cause and effect, the past and the future, the goals of life, and the sort of person who was worthy of admiration. Likewise, had we asked them what they talked about while they were engaged in rough and tumble with their children, we may well have found that they talked about the pleasures of social contact, the importance of closeness and dependence, and the importance of affiliation and how it could be promoted. We might have found them recalling past experiences and anticipating the future. In other words, as the author has argued more fully elsewhere (Raven 1977), it may be absurd to assess the tendency to engage in competent behaviour except in relation to goals the individual values.

Discipline Expectations

Figure 5.7 shows that the home visitors have, in line with their objectives, led the parents to shift from punishing their children physically toward giving more reasons and explanations, but they have not quite got there! The parents end up shouting at their children!

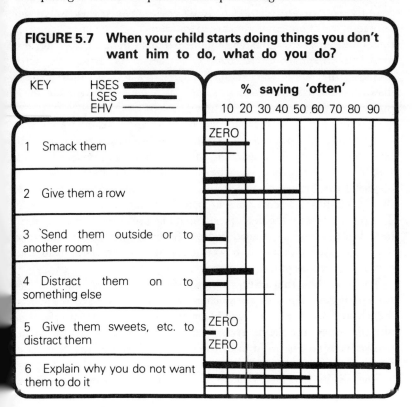

FIGURE 5.7   When your child starts doing things you don't want him to do, what do you do?

KEY   HSES
       LSES
       EHV

% saying 'often'
10 20 30 40 50 60 70 80 90

1 Smack them   ZERO

2 Give them a row

3 Send them outside or to another room

4 Distract them on to something else

5 Give them sweets, etc. to distract them   ZERO / ZERO

6 Explain why you do not want them to do it

The Wider Social Context

We have already attempted to set language activities in the context of other activities which parents might undertake with their children with a view to promoting the growth of their general competence.

We have seen that the language activities which so sharply differentiate HSES from LSES parents are only part of a wider context which involves parents' perceptions of the qualities they think it is important for their children to develop, their values, and the demands of the wider environment in which they live and work.

One perspective on the cause of the differences between HSES and LSES parents is that they are, at least in part, a product of the wider differences in the environments in which they live and work. It has been argued that these force LSES parents to spend more time operating at a lower level in Maslow's (1954) hierarchy. Another perspective holds that if the parents were prepared to engage in cognitive activity in relation to those environments, they would not only improve those environments so that they became better places for their children to grow and develop, the parents would, by so doing, also model for their children cognitive processes in action, cognitive processes that were in fact enabling them to reach their valued goals as distinct from using the school system as a means of avoiding those problems.

In order to explore this issue, parents were first asked how important they considered various features of their socio-physical environment to be. Then they were asked how satisfied they were on each count. Finally they were asked what they thought would happen if they tried to tackle the 'problem' revealed by their having rated one feature of their socio-physical environment both important and unsatisfactory. The results of only the final question will be presented in tabular form here, but the results obtained from the first two questions must first be discussed. Before doing so, however, it is useful to give the reader an overall impression of the outcome.

The data show that LSES parents do indeed have different priorities from their environments, are much more dissatisfied with those environments, and feel much less confident and competent that they will be able to cope with them. They tend to have negative self-images as people who have no right to be listened to and whose views are not to be taken seriously.

The EHVs had a significant impact on the parents' priorities in relation to their socio-physical environment, and they led them to feel better motivated to tackle their problems. Nevertheless they did not lead them to feel better *able* to tackle those problems.

I would myself argue that it is particularly important for home visitors to address themselves to this problem. By doing so, they would make it possible for parents to spend more time with their children in activities that are likely to be psychologically developing. They would make it possible for the environments in which the children grow up to be improved. And they would make it possible for parents to demonstrate to their children that cognitive activity is an important ingredient in enabling them to lead their life as they would like to lead it. I would further argue that they would enable parents to come to terms with some of the civic and social perceptions that represent barriers to our society tackling many of the problems that beset them. One cannot, for example, establish educational programmes that enable all pupils to develop their talents if one believes, as most of the parents whom we interviewed did believe, that all pupils should be treated in the same way.

There were major differences between the HSES and LSES groups' priorities in relation to the socio-physical environment. For the HSES group, the most important things were to get on well with their children, to get on well with their close family, to have schools that offered a wide variety of courses, to have teachers who took their views seriously, be able to communicate well with other people, to be on good terms with their children's teachers, to have a doctor who really listened to them, and to live in a society that made an effort to make the best use of everyone's talents and abilities.

For the low-status group, things were very different. Although they did indeed attach importance to being able to get on with their children and their close family, these things were very quickly followed by a felt need to be able to learn how to cope with their children (notice the relevance to our repeated assertion that they seem to have more difficulty coping with their children), a felt need to be able to cope with their day-to-day activities more effectively, and to live in a community in which everyone played their part in curbing vandalism.

Attention may be drawn to the fact that, while the HSES group appears to be preoccupied with relationships and services – relationships with husbands, doctors, planners, teachers, and the wider society in general – the LSES group seem to be preoccupied with getting a firmer grip on life in the here and now. They need to get control over their children, to cope with their day-to-day problems, and to get control over the vandals who plague them. This precarious nature of their lives emerges in their answers to many other questions – their children are more likely to be led into deviant behaviour; it is more important to ensure that they are fed; it is more important to find a way of ensuring that there is someone at home to look after them. Put in another way the data suggest that the LSES parents in general are trying to get a grip on satisfactions at a lower level in Maslow's hierarchy – and therefore have less *time*, whatever their inclinations, for the niceties of child-rearing. Thus our first problem may be to help them to handle these basic problems. If we did this, they might then progress naturally to the wider concerns evident in the responses of the HSES group.

But perhaps the most striking lesson to be drawn is that home visitors have, in no way, been able to lead the LSES parents to share the priorities of the HSES parents. If getting on well with husbands and relatives is an important precursor to good psychological development on the part of the children, then the visited parents have a long way to go. The same applies if children's psychological development is associated with their parents attaching importance to being able to communicate well with other people, or believing that it is important for their school system and society to develop and utilize people with a wide variety of talents. Likewise, if 'self-esteem' is taken to involve thinking that one has a right to be listened to, then the parents' responses to the items which ask whether they think it is important to have doctors, teachers, planners and officials who take their views seriously suggest that the parents' self-images still leave something to be desired. They appear to be self-depreciating, and their replies almost suggest that they do not think that their views are *worthy* of consideration. Furthermore, if one does not think that it is importa to have doctors, teachers, planners and officials who listen to one and take one's views seriously, there is really very little point in developing initiative, self-confidence, the ability to think for oneself, the ability to communicate, or concern with the wider community. The same is true if one does not feel that it is important to be able to influence what happens in one's country. And, if one does not think it is important to have opportunities to develop one's mind and learn new things as an adult, can one really be expected to place great store in the intrinsic value of educational activity at school level?

Such reflections again remind one of Maslow's (1954) hierarchy of needs and lead one to ponder its validity. If people are spending time – are forced to spend time – satisfying needs low in their hierarchy, *can* they simultaneously be concerned with needs higher up in the hierarchy? Or is the explanation of the hierarchy not that the higher level needs cannot be pursued until lower level needs have been satisfied, but that some people are incapable of or uninterested in pursuing the supposedly higher level needs? If their low-level needs are satisfied *do* they move on to a concern with the so-called higher level needs? Quite clearly, from the data we have presented, the way in which one would design a home-visiting programme is dependent on the way in which one answers these questions. And evaluation of the differential consequences of home-visiting programmes predicted on these alternative answers would yield the basic data that are needed to answer the questions.

The data on the perceived consequences of trying to do something about a complaint are presented in Figure 5.8.

The LSES group were, in general, less likely than the HSES group to say that, in trying to tackle their problems, they would be working for the long-term good of society, enjoy learning what needed to be learned in order to do it, enjoy the company of others while doing it, enjoy

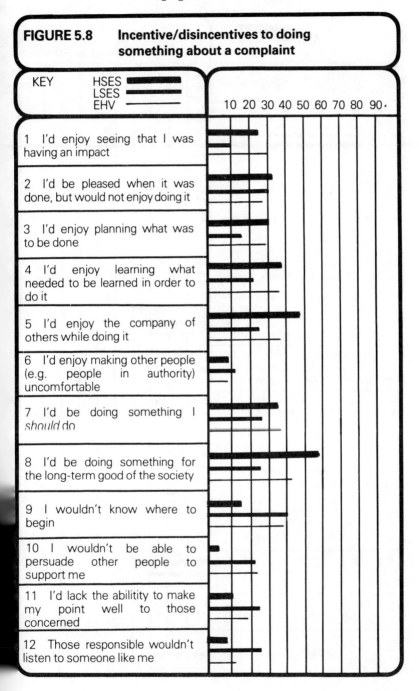

FIGURE 5.8   Incentive/disincentives to doing something about a complaint

KEY   HSES ▬▬▬
       LSES ▬▬▬
       EHV ————

10 20 30 40 50 60 70 80 90

1 I'd enjoy seeing that I was having an impact

2 I'd be pleased when it was done, but would not enjoy doing it

3 I'd enjoy planning what was to be done

4 I'd enjoy learning what needed to be learned in order to do it

5 I'd enjoy the company of others while doing it

6 I'd enjoy making other people (e.g. people in authority) uncomfortable

7 I'd be doing something I *should* do

8 I'd be doing something for the long-term good of the society

9 I wouldn't know where to begin

10 I wouldn't be able to persuade other people to support me

11 I'd lack the ability to make my point well to those concerned

12 Those responsible wouldn't listen to someone like me

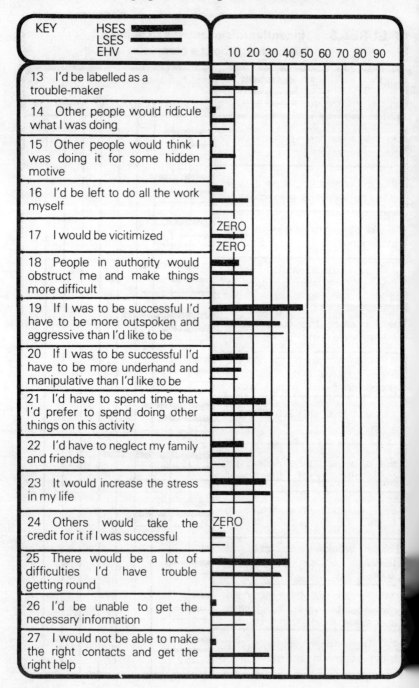

KEY   HSES ▰▰▰▰
       LSES ▬▬▬▬
       EHV ─────

10 20 30 40 50 60 70 80 90

13 I'd be labelled as a trouble-maker

14 Other people would ridicule what I was doing

15 Other people would think I was doing it for some hidden motive

16 I'd be left to do all the work myself

17 I would be vicitimized   ZERO / ZERO

18 People in authority would obstruct me and make things more difficult

19 If I was to be successful I'd have to be more outspoken and aggressive than I'd like to be

20 If I was to be successful I'd have to be more underhand and manipulative than I'd like to be

21 I'd have to spend time that I'd prefer to spend doing other things on this activity

22 I'd have to neglect my family and friends

23 It would increase the stress in my life

24 Others would take the credit for it if I was successful   ZERO

25 There would be a lot of difficulties I'd have trouble getting round

26 I'd be unable to get the necessary information

27 I would not be able to make the right contacts and get the right help

seeing that they were having an impact on society, enjoy the planning activity involved in doing it and doing something they felt they should do (i.e. something moral). On the other hand they were more likely to say that they would not know where to begin, that they would not be able to persuade other people to support them, that they would lack the ability to make their points well to those concerned, that they would not be able to get the necessary information, that those responsible would not listen to them, and that they would be labelled as trouble-makers.

All of these differences suggest that the LSES parents would be much less likely than HSES parents to do anything about their problems. They feel they lack abilities that they would need, they would be less likely to enjoy the intellectual and social activities involved, other people would be less likely to support them and, in particular, they are less likely to feel that they would be engaged in moral activity that would be in the long term interest of society. They are clearly a great deal less well motivated to do anything about their problems.

The home visitors have changed some of these perceptions and expectations. The parents who have had home visits are more likely than their LSES counterparts to feel that they would be working for the long-term good of society, and that they would enjoy both the intellectual and social activity involved in trying to do something about their problems. However, their subjective abilities have actually deteriorated. They are slightly *more* likely to say that they would not know where to begin, that they would not be able to make the right contacts, that they would not be able to persuade other people to support them, that they would not be able to make their point well, and that they would be unable to get the necessary information.

It has been suggested that these changed perceptions and expectations are purely a product of improved social contacts, independently of the other things the EHVs have done. It seems to us highly likely, both from our interviews with home-visited parents and from our previous work, that the home visitors *do* reduce the loneliness of the mothers. But, although it may be a necessary condition for it, is it responsible for the growth in confidence and competence that is documented in Figure 5.8? It seems to us that most likely it is not. More important would seem to be a process that goes on in parallel with the process of befriending the mother and extending her range of social contacts. This involves the EHV working jointly with the mother to find ways of solving the mother's particular problems. This is not a teacher-taught, or expert–novice relationship because – in this respect – the home visitor is as ignorant as the mother. Rather it is a joint problem-solving task. The same is even more true in the Leicester Home Start project, where the visitor may well come from a similar social and educational background to the mother who is visited. Such joint problem-solving activity, in which two equally ignorant people struggle to find a solution to a common problem, seems much more likely to promote the development of feelings of confidence and competence – and the ability to make one's own observations, evolve new constructs, study cause and effect, and generally think for oneself – than a teacher-taught relationship, although it may well be 'less efficient' than instruction from an expert. However, as everyday experience, and Van der Eyken's evaluation of Leicester Home Start (1981) in particular suggests, the experts are only too often wrong – because they know too little about the constraints that operate in a given situation.

So, at last, the dilemma is clear. Our data strongly suggest that, in their expert role as promoters of child development, the EHVs may be leading the parents they visit to feel *less* confident and competent. They influence the parents' attitudes and beliefs – but the parents do not take up the activities modelled by these experts. In their unprofessional role, in an area in which they are as ignorant as the mothers, they lead the mothers to feel more confident, and better motivated. Unfortunately, we do not know whether they are more likely to follow this through into action.

Despite the need to separate the loneliness issue from the competence issue, nothing we have said should be construed to mean that we think the question of social isolation is unimportant. Quite the contrary. One of the problems that has not been solved to everyone's satisfaction involves finding a way in which Educational Home Visitors can help the parents they visit to establish a social network so that they can cease to be so dependent on the home visitors themselves and so that they have a continuing support network after visiting ceases. It is clear that the solution currently being tried out – which involves the mother becoming a 'Mother Home Visitor', joining a parents' group, or visiting the nursery – may help, but that these solutions have not yet been fully exploited.

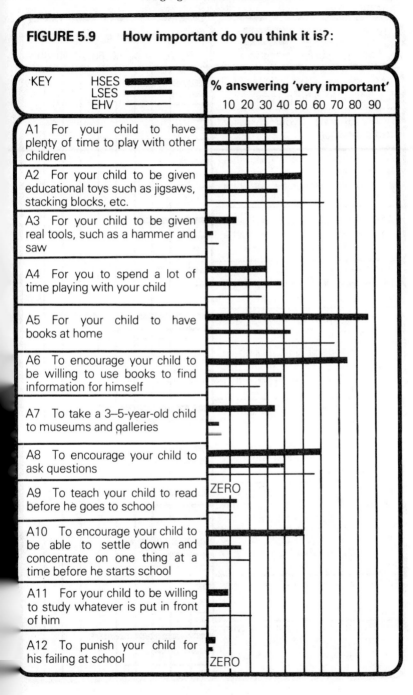

FIGURE 5.9   How important do you think it is?:

KEY   HSES
       LSES
       EHV

% answering 'very important'
10 20 30 40 50 60 70 80 90

A1 For your child to have plenty of time to play with other children

A2 For your child to be given educational toys such as jigsaws, stacking blocks, etc.

A3 For your child to be given real tools, such as a hammer and saw

A4 For you to spend a lot of time playing with your child

A5 For your child to have books at home

A6 To encourage your child to be willing to use books to find information for himself

A7 To take a 3–5-year-old child to museums and galleries

A8 To encourage your child to ask questions

A9 To teach your child to read before he goes to school   ZERO

A10 To encourage your child to be able to settle down and concentrate on one thing at a time before he starts school

A11 For your child to be willing to study whatever is put in front of him

A12 To punish your child for his failing at school   ZERO

KEY	HSES ▬▬▬ LSES ▬▬▬ EHV ————	**% answering 'very important'** 10 20 30 40 50 60 70 80 90
A13 For your child to spend a lot of time with his parents		
A14 To punish your child for bad behaviour		
A15 To teach your child that his mother has a life of her own as well and cannot be with him all the time		
A16 For your child to spend time in the company of adults who handle responsibility well		
A17 For your child to learn how to get people in authority to do what he wants them to do		
A18 For you to talk to your child a lot		
A19 To spend time talking to your child about what his interests are and what he wants out of life		
A20 To teach your child to think for himself		
A21 To teach your child that you don't get anything you want without working for it		
A22 To teach your child not to do just what's good for him but what's good for everybody		
A23 To help your child to think clearly about what he's trying to do		
A24 For you to help him only occasionally when help was really needed		
A25 For you to treat him with respect as an individual in his own right who is entitled to pursue his interests and ideas		

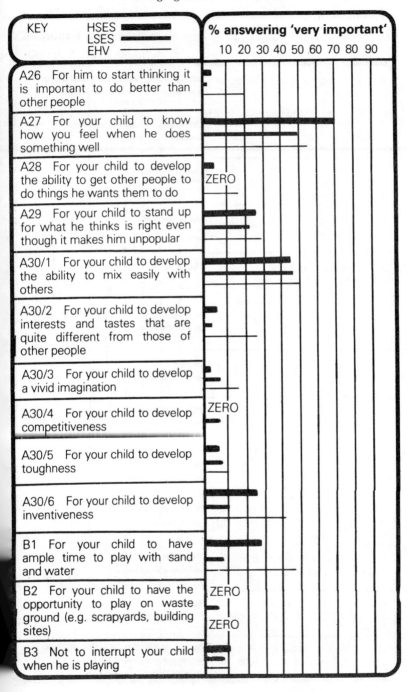

KEY	% answering 'very important'
HSES	10 20 30 40 50 60 70 80 90
LSES	
EHV	

A26   For him to start thinking it is important to do better than other people

A27   For your child to know how you feel when he does something well

A28   For your child to develop the ability to get other people to do things he wants them to do — ZERO

A29   For your child to stand up for what he thinks is right even though it makes him unpopular

A30/1   For your child to develop the ability to mix easily with others

A30/2   For your child to develop interests and tastes that are quite different from those of other people

A30/3   For your child to develop a vivid imagination

A30/4   For your child to develop competitiveness — ZERO

A30/5   For your child to develop toughness

A30/6   For your child to develop inventiveness

B1   For your child to have ample time to play with sand and water

B2   For your child to have the opportunity to play on waste ground (e.g. scrapyards, building sites) — ZERO — ZERO

B3   Not to interrupt your child when he is playing

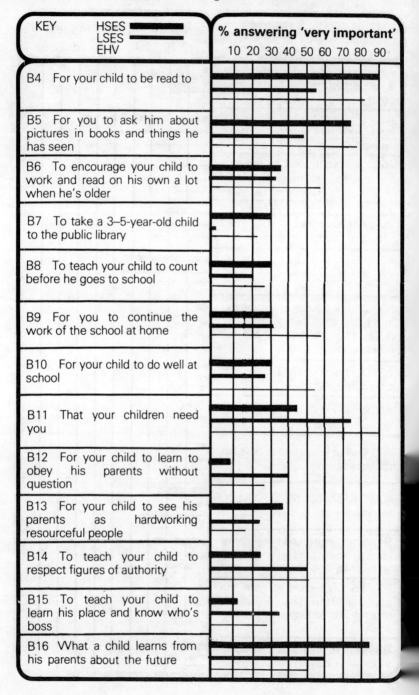

KEY HSES LSES EHV

% answering 'very important'
10 20 30 40 50 60 70 80 90

B4 For your child to be read to

B5 For you to ask him about pictures in books and things he has seen

B6 To encourage your child to work and read on his own a lot when he's older

B7 To take a 3–5-year-old child to the public library

B8 To teach your child to count before he goes to school

B9 For you to continue the work of the school at home

B10 For your child to do well at school

B11 That your children need you

B12 For your child to learn to obey his parents without question

B13 For your child to see his parents as hardworking resourceful people

B14 To teach your child to respect figures of authority

B15 To teach your child to learn his place and know who's boss

B16 What a child learns from his parents about the future

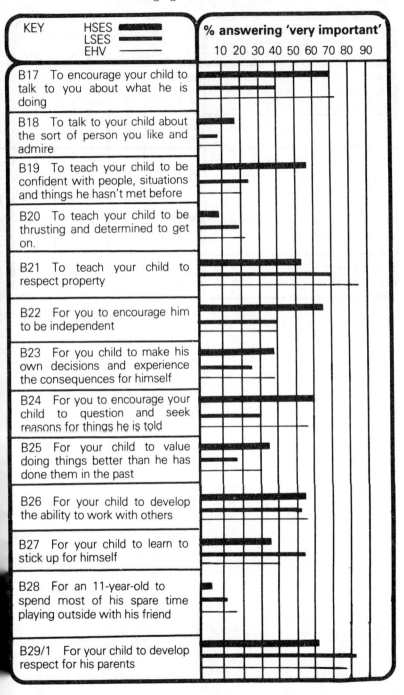

KEY   HSES
      LSES
      EHV

% answering 'very important'
10 20 30 40 50 60 70 80 90

B17 To encourage your child to talk to you about what he is doing

B18 To talk to your child about the sort of person you like and admire

B19 To teach your child to be confident with people, situations and things he hasn't met before

B20 To teach your child to be thrusting and determined to get on.

B21 To teach your child to respect property

B22 For you to encourage him to be independent

B23 For you child to make his own decisions and experience the consequences for himself

B24 For you to encourage your child to question and seek reasons for things he is told

B25 For your child to value doing things better than he has done them in the past

B26 For your child to develop the ability to work with others

B27 For your child to learn to stick up for himself

B28 For an 11-year-old to spend most of his spare time playing outside with his friend

B29/1 For your child to develop respect for his parents

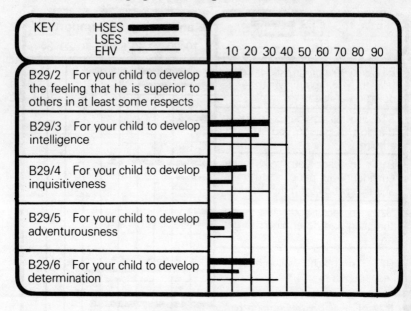

KEY   HSES ▬▬
           LSES ▬▬
           EHV ─────

10 20 30 40 50 60 70 80 90

B29/2   For your child to develop the feeling that he is superior to others in at least some respects

B29/3   For your child to develop intelligence

B29/4   For your child to develop inquisitiveness

B29/5   For your child to develop adventurousness

B29/6   For your child to develop determination

6

Assessing Language in the Home

RUTH CLARK

If the reader is expecting to be told how to assess language in the home, I am afraid he will be disappointed. When I was asked to present a paper on this topic, after some consideration I decided that all I could do in good faith was to argue that assessing language in the home is a very difficult endeavour, and perhaps not a worthwhile one. The purpose of this paper will be to point out some of the difficulties. Perhaps people will consider this a rather negative approach. Maybe there has to be assessment in certain situations, for certain purposes. In that case, I am afraid that for the time being I shall have to leave it to more constructive people to make positive recommendations as to how it may validly be done. All I can do here is draw their attention to some of the problems they will have to overcome.

I shall also argue that assessing language in the home is better, though very little better than assessing it elsewhere.

I propose to take each key word in the title in turn. to explore the implications of the process, 'assessing'; the object, 'language' and the place, 'the home'. The title does not state whose language is being assessed, but I am assuming it is the language of the pre-school child.

Assessment

The term 'assessment' typically carries with it certain implications. Assessment is standardized. By that I mean that standard material is presented according to a standard procedure, the responses are marked in terms of an objective specification of correctness, and the score evaluated against a set of norms, validated on a large population.

Typically, also, the assessment aims to specify the amount of some variable that the testee has possession of. If the assessment is developmental, the commodity is often, though not always, felt to be increasing gradually with age.

I shall take each of these aspects in turn and try to show that it is difficult to apply them to the assessment of language in a pre-school child.

To begin with, consider the notion of standard material – standard input utterances in comprehension tests and standard situations to elicit production. But each young child has his own range of experiences and his own repertoire of language items. These may be derived in an idosyncratic way from adult speech. The child hears something said, has something on his own mind, and brings the adult form, or what he can grasp of it, together with his own concept to construct a unique means of expression (Ferrier 1978; Halliday 1975; Clark 1975a, 1978). Or he may have an idea in his mind and no canonical form in his repertoire to express it, so he uses his limited resources creatively to manufacture his own individual means of expression (Braine 1974; Clark 1974).

Consider the following two incidents, examples of speech production and comprehension respectively, and contemplate how pre-established test items could legislate for their occurrence:

David (aged 2 years 9 months)
Sitting in the back of a stationary car with his mother sitting beside him, holding his baby sister on her lap. A neighbour (myself) talking to him through the window says 'Where's mummy?' A look of concentration on the child's face. As mother later explained, he apparently was trying to say that mummy usually sat at the front. She happened to be at the back that day because the baby's car seat had recently broken, so she had to hold her. It would have been beyond David's current linguistic resources to say 'Mummy usually sits at the front', but nothing daunted, he produced 'Mummy there' pointing to her, then 'Mummy *do* at front'.

Louise (aged 1 year 4 months)
In a grocer's shop, she is eating a packet of crisps, but sees her mother buying some sweets. She reaches out towards them as they go into mother's shopping bag, squeaking excitedly. 'You've got your crisps' says mum. 'You can't have the sweets till later.' Whereupon Louise hands back the half empty packet of crisps to the shop assistant over the counter. It is impossible to say how much of the verbal message was literally understood, but she certainly had a clear grasp of the logic of the situation.

Surely to base an assessment of a young child's language ability on his responses to a standard set of items, which may have no meaning for him personally, and to mark his responses according to some prior scheme of correctness, is to miss the moments when the child is communicating most effectively.

Standard Presentation

If I am right that a child's response to standard material is of no particular relevance to his ability to communicate, what of the context in which such standard material is normally presented?

Any interaction between two people is complex. As well as the ostensible meaning of an utterance, we need to consider the intention of the speaker in producing it, whether the hearer has interpreted it the way the speaker intended, whether the hearer learns from the utterance incidental facts about the speaker that it was not part of his intention to communicate, the speaker's awareness of the hearer's reaction to his communication and so on (Goffman 1957). As well as operating at all these levels simultaneously, interactions also have a temporal structure. Each participant brings a context to the interaction, and these contexts are negotiated and modified in the light of further events, as the conversation unfolds (Cook-Gumperz and Gumperz 1978).

Despite the rich texture of interactions, testers and experimenters have tended to construe testing and experimental situations in flat mechanical terms. The subject is seen as some sort of robust machine, whose behaviour is unaffected by subtle, or even fairly gross modifications in environmental conditions, and whose potentialities can be identified by pulling the appropriate levers and pressing the proper buttons. The machine will then emit certain behaviours that can be recorded objectively.

But human subjects are not inert material waiting to be operated on. They are active construers of situations. Pretending that this underlying mental activity does not exist and limiting its overt expression cannot prevent it from occurring (Bannister and Bott 1973).

Testing and experimental procedures in psychology rest on two assumptions: that behaviour under formal observation is in some sense representative of normal behaviour, and that it is unaffected by the subject's interpretation of the situation. These assumptions have been strongly challenged by the work of Orne and his associates (Orne 1973). Under experimental conditions subjects consent to perform very boring, apparently meaningless and even dangerous and antisocial acts. People's willingness to co-operate and tolerate deception and even discomfort arises from a sense of commitment to the task, and a desire to be a 'good subject' and produce the kind of behaviour that they think the experimenter requires. But the nature of this behaviour depends on the subject's perception of what Orne calls the 'demand characteristics' of the experiment. Orne sees participation in an experiment as a problem-solving task for the subject, who tries to understand the purposes of the experiment and act accordingly.

Cicourel has pursued a similar line of thought in relation to school children. He criticizes testing procedures for failing to take account of the insights of cognitive psychology. The concept of a standard situation cannot stand up to what we know about the influence of attention and other cognitive processes on the experience of situations. Cicourel sees a need to recognize and examine the gulf between teachers' and testers' interpretations of situations, and interpretations the children impose on them (Cicourel 1974).

But, you may argue, pre-school children are hardly likely to be modifying their behaviour in accordance with what they perceive to be the 'demand characteristics' of test or experimental situations. Surely they will be behaving naturally, and making no concessions to the observer's requirements. But perfectly natural behaviour is not what is required either. In a formal test situation there are certain constraints, imposed by the tester, within which the subject is required to operate. The responses of the subject will only be meaningful to the tester if the subject has conformed to those constraints.

It seems that we are in difficulties whatever happens. If the child fails to adjust his behaviour to the test situation, then he is not accepting the necessary constraints. If he is attempting to adapt to the situation, he may be misinterpreting it, and this will be just as damaging for our interpretation of the results.

It is likely that the capacity to adapt to the bizarre requirements of testing situations is slow to develop. Compare the following examples provided by a 2-year-old and by somewhat older, nursery school-age children. The first child, the 2-year-old, is making no concessions to the testing situation at all. The nursery school children either are, or are not, but in either case the results are likely to be misleading to the tester.

(1) 'Adam' we asked, 'which is right, "two shoes" or "two shoe"?' His answer, produced with explosive enthusiasm was: 'Pop goes the weasel!' (Brown and Bellugi 1964).

(2) A 4-year-old had just come out of an interview with a head-master, who was assessing his fitness for admission to the school. His mother was reprimanding him for not having answered the headmaster's questions, although she knew he knew the answers. 'If that man didn't know', said the boy indignantly, 'I wasn't going to tell him' (Roger Wales, personal communication). The boy was here demonstrating his failure to accept the formal constraints of the testing situation by not recognizing the altered function of questions in that context.

(3) In standard Piagetian number conservation tasks children accept that two rows of objects with equal numbers in each row are

equivalent. Then the objects in one row are spread out. Typically children in the pre-operational stage then say that the rows are unequal, the longer row having more objects in it. However, McGarrigle and Donaldson, testing children aged 4 and 5, showed that children only made these misjudgements if it was the experimenter who altered the length of the row, not if a 'naughty teddy' was responsible (1975). These children were showing that they were affected by the formal nature of the testing situation, and were apparently reacting to what they perceived as its 'demand characteristics'.

Another point to bear in mind about testing a young subject, 'naïve' about the structure and assumptions of test situations, is that one may be training him in the process of testing him. He may gradually come to adapt his behaviour to the formal constraints of the situation. He is learning to play a new game with language in collaboration with the tester. Looked at in this way, tests may have a value as measures of what Vygotsky (1962) has called 'the zone of proximal development'. What is being tested is the child's ability to establish a new set of behaviours in response to a demand, not a pre-existent competence. Some intelligence testing incorporates practice to see whether the child's level can be raised in the course of the testing (Tuddenham 1971).

But there is another feature of formal testing and experimental situations that needs to be reappraised in the light of a closer knowledge of what actually goes on when children are learning to speak. This is the process of controlling variables. In scientific investigations researchers strip away irrelevant variables, either by holding them absolutely constant, or ensuring that they range across a comparable set of values in the groups or conditions being compared. The purpose of these procedures is to ensure that any effect observed can be attributed unambiguously to the variable that the experimenter has manipulated.

But the more one exercises control in this fashion, the more different the situation is to what the child is used to, and the more baffled he is likely to be as a result. If you restrict the input to a child in a comprehension test so that there is only one formal clue to a distinction in meaning, as well as preventing him from bypassing that clue to his response by depending on other clues to meaning, you are putting demands on him that he never has to meet in everyday interactions. Bridges argues that we should study natural situations in which meanings are communicated between mother and child to gain a deeper understanding of the sources of the child's comprehension, rather than presenting him with novel, rigidly structured tasks

(Bridges 1979). She shows that in such natural situations the child is given numerous and various additional clues to help him grasp his mother's meanings.

Warden also draws attention to the paradox the researcher into child language is faced with. If he wants to know precisely which linguistic structures the child has control over, he has to restrict the input so that the child must focus on these to produce a correct response, but in doing so he distorts the normal patterns of communication, and may elicit entirely spurious responses from the child, which arise from the difficulties he has in making sense of the situation (Warden 1979).

Indeed, in view of our growing knowledge about the co-operative nature of early language, the frameworks the mother provides for the child's contribution in communication games (Ratner and Bruner 1978) and in early conversations (Shugar 1978), one might argue that it is the mother–child dyad that one ought to be testing, rather than assessing one member of the pair independently, isolated from the normal context of interaction.

Objective Marking

The preoccupation that psychologists have with objectivity and scientific procedures has influenced research into child language through the use of controlled experimentation. The objective procedures of linguistics, on the other hand, seem to have influenced child language research in the sphere of examining the linguistic outputs of the child. It is in relation to these procedures that we need to consider the feasibility of marking objectively in language tests for pre-school children.

A number of investigators of child language have shown a reluctance to attribute understanding of a linguistic concept to a child unless they can identify some clear-cut overt marker of that understanding. To take an early example, Brown and Fraser (1964) went to great lengths to establish that 'here' and 'there' were members of the same grammatical class in Adam's speech, by calculating the proportion of contexts that they shared. They came to the intriguing conclusion that 'here' shared more contexts with 'there' than 'here' in the first half of the corpus shared with 'here' in the second part of the corpus. This procedure highlights the problem of whether we should let our own intuitions intrude into studies of linguistic material, or whether we should rely purely on objective measures. Brown and Fraser tried to have their cake and eat it, since clearly they would never have compared 'here' with 'there' in the first place unless they had some reason to suppose that they were related in meaning.

We now have a much fuller awareness of the inescapability of making interpretations of the child's meaning in studies of children's speech, though we are no nearer attaining fully specified procedures for identifying meaning, that are interchangeable between observers. But even in much more recent discussions of children's understanding, the very people that have argued most convincingly for making rich interpretations that go beyond what is actually expressed in the child's utterance (Brown 1973; Bloom 1970) are still reluctant to abandon totally a dependence on overt markers as a basis for inference about children's intentions. They cling to them in relation to certain issues about intention, having abandoned them in relation to other issues. For example Brown claims that 'the appropriate word order is the prime aspect of the child's early sentences that justifies our attributing to him the intention to communicate certain semantic roles or relations' (Brown 1973, p. 41). Bloom will only attribute the mastery of a grammatical relation to a child if he programmes his utterance as a unit, integrated in one intonation contour, rather than as a successive one word utterance (Bloom 1973).

As I pointed out in a review of Bloom's book *One Word at a Time*

> The inconvenient fact seems to be that there is no one-to-one relationship in children's speech between the intention to express relational meaning and either an integrated prosodic contour or stable word order. Children produce utterances with the prosodic contour and some of the syntactic features of adult utterances but without any underlying relational meaning (Clark, Hutcheson and Van Buren 1974). . . . Children produce utterances that clearly express relational meaning without the help of either a prosodic contour or stable word order, e.g. the successive, single-word utterance 'hold, hand, hold, hand, hold, hand, hold, hand' (Clark *et al*. 1974) Clark 1975b.

As Huttenlocher points out 'Although a broad consensus has developed that the important questions about language development concern the relation of the linguistic code to the mental representation of events, many of the implications of this position remain to be worked out' (Huttenlocher 1974). If we are concerned to understand how a child develops concepts, how he acquires the forms of his language, and how he learns the links between particular concepts and forms, we have to treat the concepts and the forms as being capable of being acquired independently. We cannot take one as the measure of the other if we are trying to discover how one comes to represent the other. The easiest way to measure the development of concepts is to assume that the emergence of a form signals the emergence of the corresponding concept, but we know from numbers of research projects on semantic development that for many concepts this is not the case. We cannot assume it is for any concept without independent evidence. If something is difficult to measure we can pretend it does not exist or measure it by some inadequate means which happens to be convenient. This is common practice in psychology. But it is hardly a satisfactory procedure.

These considerations raise untold difficulties for the objective marking of linguistic responses in assessments of child language development.

Another source of confusion about the meaning of children's utterances is that they do not always mean what they say. Utterances may have functions other than the communication of meaning. For example, Steffensen (1978) has shown that children's answers to questions may be devices for coping with their own lack of comprehension, and attention to their ostensible meaning will just mislead the researcher. Blank (1974) suggests that the function of *why* questions at a certain stage is not to seek information about the causes of events, but to explore the meaning of the word 'why' which the child has not yet grasped. Such phenomena would be a source of noise in a formal asssessment system, and it could only be hoped that they would not completely drown the reverberations of true competence.

As well as these problems about what evidence signals mastery of a concept, we still have the same problems arising from the idiosyncratic and personal nature of a child's language which we had in relation to standard experimental material. In order to understand what a child means by a particular utterance one may need to have some special knowledge of his past experience. On one occasion, when recording a child's speech, I was able to make sense of an utterance that baffled the child's mother, because I happened to have been present the previous day when a related incident occurred. The child had been looking at a picture book with me in which a Teddy bear was burning leaves on a bonfire. I touched the fire and pretended to have been burnt. David aged 2 years and 8 months, said 'sore hand'. Next day when I started to play the same game with him it suddenly occurred to him to grab my hand and push it against the fire saying 'my sore hand'. In the light of the previous incident, it seem clear that he was using 'sore' as a causative 'make sore'. The pronoun 'my' was his word for 'me'. interpreted the utterance to mean 'Let me make the hand sore'. But if had not been present on the previous day, and remembered the incident well because I had transcribed the tape between visits, I think it very unlikely that I could have made any sense of it at all.

Sometimes even very close association with a child over a considerable period of time is no guarantee that his speech will be intelligible. There would be little point in giving an example of an unintelligible utterance, since there would be nothing interesting I could say about it. However, an example of a word whose origin was for some time obscure, and an example of a situation whose significance remained obscure for a number of years might serve to illustrate the problem.

Over a period of some months during his third year Adam used the word 'intit' to mean elephant. He was quite impervious to correction, and we could find no reason for the error until one day I happened to be playing over an earlier tape recording, which had been transcribed and checked without the incident being noticed at the time. A visitor was in the house, looking at a book with Adam. At one point he said 'That's an elephant isn't it'. 'Intit' repeated Adam. And that is how the elephant got its name.

A situation that was not fully understood until about four years later occurred during a recording session when Ivan was intermittently, during the whole twenty minutes of the session, tapping out letters on a typewriter, and drawing shapes on a piece of paper alongside shapes drawn by Sandy, the visiting phonetician. The adults seemed concerned for him to type his name on a fresh piece of paper.

He again and again pressed for a pencil. He wanted to write his name. He was preoccupied with the question as to who had drawn which shapes. Ivan had the adults' full attention for much of the time, but they totally failed to grasp that the situation had for him a unifying theme which completely eluded them. Only on playing the recording over twice some three years later for the purpose of an analysis to be described below did it suddenly dawn on me that uppermost in his mind the whole time had been the practice of writing in the corner of a drawing done at the nursery school the name of the child who had drawn it. He wanted his name to be written on his drawing and her name to be written on her drawing.

If so much can escape observers with a special interest in the child's speech, and sound recordings to mull over, how much of a child's meaning must inevitably escape the observer in an isolated formal test session.

Underlying Scales

The last feature of standardized tests that I shall consider is the structure and pattern of growth they attribute to the variable they are measuring. The traditional focus is on the measurement on a single scale of some commodity that some people are held to possess in greater abundance than others and which, during childhood, is assumed to be increasing gradually in amount (Ryan 1972). Another approach aims at drawing up a profile of abilities (e.g. Elliot, Murray and Pearson 1978). Neither of these ways of conceptualizing the process of development could readily accommodate individual differences in strategies of learning, nor sharp transitions between stages of development. Yet it seems that language development exhibits these features.

In a major pioneer study of language development beginning in the late 1950s three children took part. Even in such a small sample as this two separate ways of contrasting styles of the learners have been proposed. Brown saw Adam's way of speaking as different to that of Eve and Sarah. Adam, he argued, made more errors of commission than the other two (Brown 1968). (Though he did dismiss the difference as superficial. Adam gave a rich print-out but there was no difference in underlying competence.) Cazden, on the other hand, identified differences between the patterns of Eve and Sarah's learning (Cazden 1968). She called Eve's pattern 'macrodevelopment'. Eve was trying to say more complex things, but without accurate syntax. Sarah's pattern she called 'microdevelopment'. Sarah was capable of expressing her less elaborate intentions in a grammatical way. Bloom too (1973) has made suggestions regarding individual differences in language learning strategies. Some children, she suggests, acquire function words early on, and combine these with content words in utterances of the type that used to be described as pivot-open structures (McNeill 1968). These function words have relational meaning implicit in them, even before they combine with other words. Other children, suggests Bloom, use mainly content words in their early utterances, and relational meaning is not implicit in these words, but is only realized by their combination with other words in sequence. Limber (1973) anticipated a distinction elaborated by Nelson (1973) between 'referential' and 'expressive' speech. It is not yet clear whether this distinction is related to that made by Bloom. There are points of contact. But what is clear is that we have a great deal more to learn about individual strategies in learning language and how they affect measurable aspects of speech at various ages. Nelson's distinction has already proved fruitful in the comparison of different strategies of answering questions (Horgan 1978).

Sudden transitions in development have been reported by a number of observers. Stark (1978) has noticed in the development of infant sounds that items practised independently become integrated into more complex units and this 'may reflect a quantal jump in . .

development'. Volterra and Taeschner (1978) have described stages in the development of the language of bilinguals. Dore, Franklin, Miller and Ramer postulate discontinuity in the development of reference and syntax (1976).

But you may argue that tests of language development need not adopt the traditional models for development, but can adopt models closer to the realities of individual strategies and sharp transitions. Perhaps so, but before we could devise tests that did justice to that reality, we would need to have a much fuller knowledge of the details of these processes.

As a matter of fact, the assumptions of unitary traits and gradual growth are being challenged by concepts of 'stage' and 'strategy' in the very area where they originally arose, that of intellectual development. But the implications of these new approaches for testing have not yet been spelt out. Indeed, it is not clear whether they can be very readily. Attempts to measure stages of intellectual growth are bedevilled by disparities in level of functioning in the same child in different tasks and with different materials (Tuddenham 1971). (Attempts to use Piagetian items in the new British Intelligence Scale were thwarted by this consideration (Elliot, Murray and Pearson 1978), though Uzgiris and Hunt (1975) had more success using Piagetian stage theory to measure development in infants.) Furthermore, the very possibility of there being different stages in development complicates the measurement of individual styles of cognitive functioning (Entwistle 1979). In short, the measurers of cognitive development are not yet in a position to help us with problems of measuring language development according to its true nature, any more than we are yet sufficiently certain what that true nature is.

Language

In previous sections I argued that the apparatus of formal assessment is inappropriate for monitoring the language development of the pre-school child. In this section I shall argue that a further difficulty is that we have not yet decided what we mean by language. Views fluctuate as to what material is relevant to a study of language development. For example, in the not too distant past investigators were leaving imitations out of their analyses of the child's speech, apparently from a theoretical conviction that these were unimportant, since they did not reflect the creative functioning of the child's own competence (Bloom 1970, p. 17). From certain claims based on more recent investigations it seems that imitations may be a very important feature of child language, throwing light on the growth of syntax, semantics, and pragmatics (Clark 1977; Ferrier 1978; Keenan 1974; Ryan 1973).

Similarly, theoretical issues influence judgements as to when language begins. For example, a pragmatic framework for viewing child language will regard use of early words with fluid meaning as an important phase in the mastery of communiction. Other approaches to semantic development require words to have stable meanings before analysis can proceed (Bates 1976, p. 423).

But it is not only the status of certain classes of utterance that is at issue. Recent work on comprehension treats changes in the complexity of behaviour in response to 'where' questions as crucially relevant to the development of language (Huttenlocher 1974). Huttenlocher found that children began by being able to look around and find the object named when it was in view. Only later could they go in search of a named object that was out of sight, provided it was in its usual place. Later still they could search for objects in temporary locations. Since these behaviours reflect changes in the child's capacity to represent information about objects, Huttenlocher regards them as relevant to the growth of comprehension. They could be regarded as aspects of cognitive rather than linguistic development, but the borderline between these two areas is becoming increasingly difficult to demarcate.

Further ambiguity about the nature of language is created by studies of gesture systems. Goldin-Meadows has closely observed six deaf children, of hearing parents (Goldin-Meadows 1979). These children were exposed only to spoken language, in an effort to facilitate the development of lip reading and speech. The children developed spontaneous systems of gestures in an attempt to communicate with people around them. Is this a form of language or not? It would be wrong to dismiss it as peculiar to children with a handicap. Hearing children, too, produce such gesture language (Stokoe 1977). I have records in my own data of gesture utterances. At the age of 14 months Ivan pointed his finger downwards, towards some hot tea in a cup and shook his head. I took him to be saying that one ought not to touch the tea because it was hot. Two months later, at Christmas time, he pointed to a parcel and then to himself with a questioning expression on his face. Presumably that meant 'is that for me?' Another important characteristic of these gesture utterances is that they appear to emerge before spoken words (Gardner and Gardner 1975), either because they are easier to learn than spoken words or because adults can recognize attempts at gesture signs more readily than attempts at words. It would be foolish to dismiss them as non-language, as they might ultimately throw considerable light on the human capacity for communication.

To canonize certain features of linguistic behaviour in a formal assessment scheme is to be unresponsive to the fluid nature of our understanding of the roots of communication. Language could too easily be identified with 'what language tests measure' to the impoverishment of subsequent research.

When I was discussing the possibility of using standard material in language assessment, I described a child's strategy for making herself eligible for a forbidden packet of sweets. Such incidents defy a strict demarcation between language and non-language in the behaviour of a young child. Here is another incident equally difficult to categorize and quantify. Karen, a 2-year-old, had been at the shops with her mother and a friend called Dolly, buying Karen a dress. Karen's mother had asked Dolly to take the dress meantime and bring it to the house later, when she came to tea, since she herself was burdened with other parcels. When Dolly arrived with the dress at tea-time Karen's mother asked Karen who had bought her the dress. Karen, in some sort of confusion, whether linguistic or otherwise, replied that Dolly had bought her the dress. Her mother was very upset by this. Later, when they sat down to tea, Mum proudly produced a cake, and fishing for compliments again asked Karen 'Who baked the cake?' Karen, this time understanding the situation perfectly well, with all its overtones, looked at her mother archly and proclaimed with tongue in cheek 'Dolly bake cake' (Renira Huxley, personal communication).

The Home

If a child's language is to be assessed at all, then the home is the only place to do it. I firmly believe that children produce their most elaborate speech in familiar surroundings among people with whom they are completely relaxed. We know from current work on thinking, with children and adolescents, that they produce their best performances when the material is thoroughly familiar (e.g. Peel 1978). If the complexity of a child's language is in any way related to the complexity of his thinking, then we ought to expect his language to be at its richest when he is thoroughly at home, unstressed by unfamiliar objects, surroundings and people, and therefore free to elaborate his thoughts and express them. I do have a limited amount of concrete evidence that one child, whom no one could call inhibited or shy, did nevertheless produce less advanced speech in the presence of an observer, even though that person had been visiting the home roughly once a week for nearly a year.

Ivan Clark's speech was recorded from the age of 16 months to 45 months by a variety of methods. I shall describe the three main ones here. *Continuous* recordings of twenty minutes duration were made at weekly intervals during the first phase of the study, though they were reduced to roughly once a fortnight after the period to be described here. These recordings took the usual form of periodic recording sessions described in the literature, except that they were more frequent than many, and one of the investigators was the child's mother, myself. The phonetician Sandy Hutcheson and I joined in the child's play and engaged him in conversation chatting sporadically between ourselves, while attempting to be as natural as possible. The sessions were recorded through a permanently fixed overhead microphone, a Sennheiser MD21, on to a Uher 4200 stereo tape recorder. Another Sennheiser 214 Lavalier microphone, suitable for picking up whispered comments, was on a long lead and could go anywhere in the room for me to whisper my interpretations of the child's utterances and relevant information about what was happening at the time. These were recorded on to the second track of the tape. It might appear that the whispering on the second microphone made the situation highly artificial, but this cannot account for the differences found between the language in this type of recording and the other recordings since this whispering was a common feature. Indeed, it was a perfectly natural feature of the child's life by that time, for since the beginning of the study his speech had been monitored for an average of thirty hours a week using this same apparatus. During these monitored recordings sound was being recorded continually on a thirty-second loop whenever child and mother were together in the rooms with the recording facilities. These were the two main rooms in the house, where most of the child's daily activity took place when he was indoors. On a long lead, linked to the mobile microphone already mentioned, was a switch. Whenever this was pressed the tape recorder, which was out of sight in a different room, began to copy from the loop on to the upper track of the tape. Meantime comments could be whispered through the mobile microphone on to the lower track. When the switch was turned off the tape recorder switched itself off after a delay of thirty seconds (Clark 1976).

With the aid of this apparatus the child's speech and its verbal context were *monitored* for roughly thirty hours a week over the period of the study, yielding almost 150 three-quarter-hour tapes tapping roughly 900 hours of conversation. The aim was to get as complete a record of the gradual emergence of syntactic structures as possible, tracing day-to-day developments. The apparatus allows long periods of silence, adult conversation, sheer noise and utterances that have frequently been heard before to be eliminated before they are recorded on yards and yards of tape, swamping the relevant data. It would be impossibly expensive and time-consuming to record continuously over such long periods of time and daunting to search the tapes afterwards for useful data.

The aim was not to select utterances for permanent recording on any other basis but novelty of some interesting kind. It is of course extremely difficult to apply such a criterion under time pressure. It was therefore important to build in safeguards against biased sampling of the data. More than one method was used, but the one I shall describe here is the *validation* sample. Arrangements were made for the tape recorder to be set to switch itself on for two twenty-minute periods per week, according to a random schedule, which I did not know. This meant that there were times when I thought I was switching the tape recorder on and off to select items, but in fact it was on all the time. Validation recordings could then be checked to see if important events were occurring which I was failing to select.

The existence of these validation recordings will enable twenty-minute periods of conversation occurring under normal conditions (or normal for this child) to be compared with twenty-minute sessions of continuous recording in the presence of the visiting phonetician. So far I have only succeeded in comparing one continuous recording, made when Ivan was 30 months 12 days old, with one validation recording made two days later. As luck would have it, this was only fifteen minutes in length since everyone was out of the room for the first five minutes that the tape recorder was on. It is unreasonable to make too much of this comparison, since only two brief samples are being compared. However, the differences are striking, and confirm the general impression I had throughout the study that the staged recording sessions were not tapping anything like the full range of the child's linguistic repertoire.

Some details of the comparison are presented below:

Continuous sample:

Of 47 utterances in 20 minutes
    10 were one word answers
    3 were lines from songs
    5 were immediate imitations of one word or phrase,
       e.g. Sandy 'Yes, let's put it on the floor.' Ivan 'on the floor'.

There was only one question: 'Where's . . .' followed by some unintelligible item. Apparently he had lost his pen.

Negatives and modals only occurred in utterances with an 'instrumental' or 'regulatory' function (Halliday 1975), i.e. when the child was trying to influence another person's behaviour in some way, or express his own wants.

> e.g. 'Mummy, you don't do that, I do that', putting paper in the typewriter.
> 'I don't want a broken one' (a biscuit).
> 'You have to write it in there, do it in there', trying to get Sandy to write his name on the picture, rather than type it on a clean sheet of paper (see above).
> 'Can wind it', turning the roller of the typewriter.

Among other utterances with instrumental functions were 17 desideratives, but only two imperatives ('You don't do that,' and 'Do it in there', mentioned above).

> e.g. 'I want some sugar in my juice.'
> 'I want to write my name.'
> 'I want a pencil.'

The only complex sentences were joined by 'and'.

> e.g. 'That's round circles and that's seats', drawing.
> 'You made a seat there and you made a seat there and you made and I made a seat there and I made a seat there and I made a seat there.'

Validation sample:

Of 24 utterances in fifteen minutes.

There were no one-word answers or parroted lines from songs.

There were no simple imitations. In cases where material from someone else's previous utterances was imitated and used by the child something more elaborate was done to it. It was embedded in a longer utterance and distorted in some way.

> e.g. Mother: 'I'm trying to get all the things out, love', removing clothes that Ivan had put in the dining-room cupboard.
> Ivan: 'I'm trying to get all the things in.'
> Adam: (immediately after the above) 'Have you fixed it *all up*?'
> Ivan: 'I'm tidying *all up* in.'
> Father: 'Yes, tidy, tidy little chap. Hm. I'm not sure it all goes there.'
> Adam: 'So am I.' (I think he meant 'So am I tidying up'.)
> Ivan: 'It goes so am I.'

Some more complex strategies than simple imitation are at work here though they are not foolproof devices for producing grammatica

English. Ivan is 'converting' previous utterances, 'amalgamating' utterances, and 'coupling' one utterance with another (Clark 1977, 1978).

There was only one question, but far more complex than the one in the continuous sample:

'How can we put the dalek thing in there?'

Negatives and modals occurred in utterances that appeared to be more 'heuristic' (Halliday 1975), i.e. more concerned with understanding the world than with controlling other people's behaviour, though the distinction is perhaps a little tenuous here.

'That's shut, no it isn't shut', referring to the door of the cupboard.
Adam: 'Shut the door.'
Ivan: 'We don't shut the door. We don't shut my door cos it's not finished.' 'You have to throw all these in the dustbin', referring to miscellaneous papers lying about that his father had been sorting.

There were no desideratives, but a handful of imperatives:

e.g. 'Sit on my knee, and Adam sit on that, and mummy sit on this.'
'You shut your door.'
'Let's get in this boat, you get on this boat.'

There was a complex sentence using 'cos' (cited above as a negative).

The significance of some of these differences is not very clear. For example, why desideratives in one sample, imperatives in the other? Are they substituting for each other? Why does the child ask no questions in the continuous sample? But for whatever reason Ivan's speech in the two samples seems to be very different in many ways that may or may not be confirmed when further samples are compared.

It is interesting to note that other workers have also commented on variations between instrumental and regulatory uses of speech and heuristic uses. Differing claims have been made as to the order of emergence of these functions. For example, McNeill and McNeill (1968) claim, on the basis of Japanese data, that negatives are used in the function of 'denial', a heuristic function, before 'rejection', a pragmatic function. Bloom (1970) claims that both these functions of negation arise at the same time, whereas Griffiths (1979) found that the pragmatic functions of negation and affirmation – refusal, rejection, acceptance, compliance – emerged earlier than heuristic functions – denial or affirmation of other people's statements.

Clearly, it is difficult to resolve controversies like this about order of emergence until we know how far the type of language used is influenced by details of the situation. This raises similar issues to those

that preoccupy researchers into cognitive development. Do failures i
conceptual tasks reflect lack of underlying competence, or are they du
to situational effects (Bryant 1973; Donaldson 1978)?

Some readers might be tempted to dismiss the differences describe
above as idiosyncratic – peculiar to the particular people involved, an
their conduct in the recording sessions. Such readers would have
stronger case if they could produce counter-evidence, i.e. evidence tha
a child's language need not differ in a recording session from h
language in the everyday family context.

My colleagues and I also started a study in which we were intendin
to make six videotapes of the child of another member of the team, a
he played in his home. We abandoned the study after two session:
since the father judged that his son's speech was quite different froi
usual when he was being filmed, though in that instance we did n
catalogue the difference systematically.

In comparing the continuous and validation samples an estimate
differences in the language produced over similar periods of time i
different contexts can be gained. Comparisons with the monitore
sample give a different type of information. They show material that
being missed when samples of brief duration are taken. They cannot,
course, be used to show the relative frequency of more elabora
structures, since they have been selected for their interest, but tl
variety of structures that occur but are missed by the fifteen- and twent
minute samples within two days of the monitored sample is startling.

The monitored sample contains reported speech, a depende
question, yes-no questions, conditionals, an attempt at contrasti\
stress, tense used to contrast ongoing action with completed action ar
the following episodes demonstrating levels of cognitive and linguist
activity that one could be forgiven for considering to be quite beyor
the child of the continuous recording two days previously:

'Rhubarb fool, doesn't make me sick.' We had denied him an eg
because they made him sick.
'Now I can swim cos I haven't any other on my pants on.' His fath
had started to undress him.
'Dalek, you're eating an egg, that egg would, would, that egg wou
make me sick.'
'I'm a special dalek that I've got a hat on.'

Conclusion

I have argued that formal assessments of children's language, *even*
the home, are likely to misrepresent their language skills. This is tr\

for two reasons. In the first place the child will not be performing at the level he normally performs. In the second place, we do not know enough about the course of language development, or the nature of the relevant skills, to construct tests whose structure and content is appropriate. There is a further set of objections to formal testing that I have not even touched on, related to the damaging preconceptions that can be engendered by labelling children on the basis of inadequate information (Rosenthal and Jacobson 1968; Bannister and Bott 1973), but I'll let that go for now.

But what if we have to assess? I think that depends on what we are assessing for.

Suppose we are assessing children to detect early disorders of language development. Maybe we need special knowledge of the kinds of communication problem associated with different pathological conditions rather than an all-purpose instrument designed for assessing the development of normal children. For example, Menyuk has argued that so-called 'immature speech' does not merely represent a delay in development, but is qualitatively different to normal speech (1964). Fenn has criticized a recent book on normal and deficient child language for the assumption it makes that the deficient is just the normal slowed down, rather than being different in kind (1978).

Suppose we are assessing children to capture delayed language development in a normal child as early as possible, as the Bullock Report recommends (1975). Then we need details of what is going wrong and why before we can do anything to remedy it. Attempts to use assessment tools for diagnostic purposes when they have not been designed for that end are misconceived (Gathercole 1968).

Suppose we want to assess children to gauge the success of intervention programmes. Assessment procedures have to be tailor-made to the purposes of the particular programme. Also, there are good arguments for a more flexible method of evaluating educational programmes. A method that is more responsive to the realities of the different settings in which the innovation is being tried: a method that can yield insights that were not anticipated at the outset (Parlett and Hamilton 1972).

Perhaps you feel that we need assessment tools in order to learn more about the process of normal language development. But I feel that the reverse is the case. We need to know more about the process of normal language development before we can construct useful tools. And the way we will learn more, I feel, is by increasing the sensitivity of the human assessor to what goes on in situations that are as natural as possible for the communicating child.

7

Influences of the Home on
Language Development

GORDON WELLS

Perhaps the most impressive finding from the longitudinal study of language development that we have been conducting in Bristol is the very great similarity between children in the amount they have learned by the time they reach school age and in the sequence in which that learning takes place. With the possible exception of at most two children out of 128, all have developed mastery of the major meaning relations encoded in the sentence (Wells and Woll 1979) and of the syntactic structures through which they are realized, and all are using language for a wide variety of functions. It is important to stress this very broad area of similarity at the outset, since most of this paper will be concerned with the fairly narrow area in which differences between children can be observed, and I should not wish to give the impression that the differences were more important than the great similarity in their achievement.

Nevertheless, there is no doubt about the differences. On every measure on which we have compared the children, there has been substantial variation. To take just two examples: while the average Mean Length of Utterance (MLU) at 3¼ years is 4.1 morphemes, the most advanced children already have an MLU of more than 6 morphemes – a value not attained by the average child until after the age of 5 years, while the least advanced children still have an MLU of 2.2 which is the average for the sample as a whole at 2¼ years – a range of three years between most and least advanced. Similarly on other measures, where we have been able to identify a clear order in which terms in a system emerge, there is very considerable variation in the age at which particular milestones are passed. In reaching the criterion of mastery of the auxiliary verb system, for example, the average age is approximately 32 months, but the ages for individual children range from 21 to more than 42 months (Wells 1979).

One aim of our study has been to seek for possible causes of this variation in features of the children's environment, in the hope that this may be the first step towards improving the opportunities of those who are making the least satisfactory progress. Since our sample was stratified in terms of season of birth, sex and family background, it was with these three variables that we began our investigation. Probably to nobody's surprise, we found that there was no significant variation according to month of birth, although there was a trend for summer-born children to be slower developers. As far as sex is concerned, too, we found no significant variation. Although on some dimensions there was a trend for girls to be in advance of boys, including the variable of volubility, there were other dimensions on which the trend was for boys to be in advance of girls. Over all, however, the trends were fairly evenly balanced and, as already stated, they were not statistically significant. This is equally true for parents' speech to children of one sex as opposed to the other (Woll 1979).

As far as family background is concerned, the results are not so straightforward. In selecting the children in our sample, we used an index of family background that was calculated by summing the occupational status and the length of education of both parents.* The resulting scale (6–18) was then divided into four classes, A, B, C and D with scores 6–9, 10–13, 14–15 and 16–18 respectively. An equal number of children were selected to represent each of these four Classes of Family Background (FB). Each child can thus be described in terms of the class, A–D, to which he belongs or, more precisely, in terms of his score on the FB scale.

On the majority of measures of language development derived from the recordings of spontaneous speech, differences between FB Class groups do not show a consistent trend for higher scores to be significantly associated with higher status groups. In all cases differences between individuals within these groups are considerably greater than differences between the mean scores of the groups. On the other hand, when the children are compared in terms of their FB scores, although the majority of children in *all* class groups tend to score within one standard deviation either side of the sample mean, extreme scores, both high and low, tend to be distributed in such a way that high scorers are found at the upper end of the FB scale and lower scorers at the lower

---

* The formula used was FB score = Father's R.G. + Mother's R.G. + 2 (Father's Ed.) + 2 (Mother's Ed.), where R.G. = Registrar-General's 5 point scale of occupation and Ed. = Length of Education, which could be either minimal (=2) or more than minimal (=1).

end (Figure 7.1). Scores from tests administered under more controlled conditions, however, show a significant trend for children from the lower end of the FB scale to score below the sample mean. Since many of the same children achieve scores at or above the mean on measures derived from spontaneous speech, their poor test performance is attributed as much to their relative unfamiliarity with the demands of the test situation itself as to a real difference in the linguistic abilities that the tests purport to measure (Wells 1978b).

One further detail of interest emerged from this part of our investigation. Part of the questionnaire administered to the mothers when the children were aged 3½ years contained several sets of questions used by Bernstein and his colleagues in their investigation of the internal structure of the family on the dimension of 'positional' vs 'personal' organization. On the basis of the factor analysis of maternal responses to these questions, those that contributed to the factor identified with the positional–personal dimension were retained, and a score derived for each family on this dimension. As predicted, the correlation between these scores and the children's scores on the scale of family background was high ($r = .50, p < 001$). At age 3½ years, the correlations between the positional–personal index and the various linguistic indices were lower than those between the linguistic indices and family background and, in all but one case, statistically non-significant. By 5 years of age, however, the pattern was reversed: positional–personal scores were generally more highly correlated with scores on linguistic measures than were family background scores, with correlations significant in several cases at the 1 per cent level. Bernstein's hypothesis concerned the relationship between family organization and code orientation – a topic that we have not attempted to investigate. Nevertheless, the finding that, with increasing age, differences between mothers in their responses to questions about family organization came to assume greater importance than scores on the scale of family background in predicting variation in rate of linguistic development suggests that it is differences in style of interaction within the family rather than position of the family within the social hierarchy as such, that are important in accounting for children's differential success in the development of linguistic abilities. This was indeed our initial expectation and it is to the exploration of these different styles of interaction that our current work is directed.

Recent work in child language has established beyond reasonable doubt the existence of a special register adopted by parents – and other caretakers – when speaking to young children. 'Motherese', as it has been called, seems to have a number of features that may well prove to

FIGURE 7.1 Distribution of MLU(s) × Family Background Score (Age 3 years)

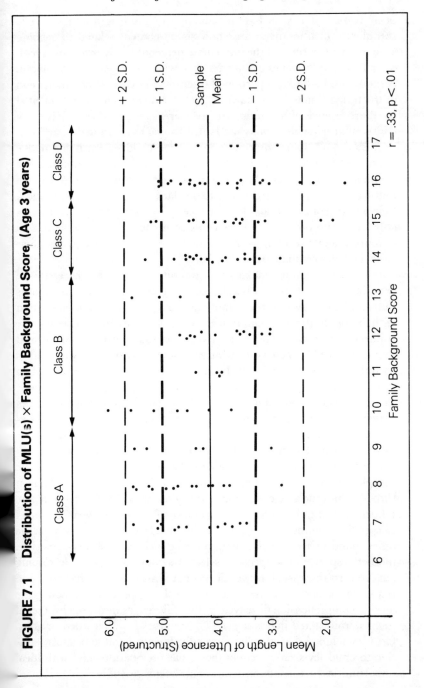

be universal. These include a reduction in the length and syntactic complexity of utterances, an emphasis on content related to ongoing activity or to features of the immediate perceptible environment, a high degree of repetitiveness, a tendency towards exaggerated intonation contours and a high proportion of utterances pitched at the higher end of the range (Snow 1977; Garnica 1977). Is this register merely elicited by the presence of an immature speaker/hearer, or does it have any consequences for development? Is it, as some have wanted to argue, a necessary and sufficient condition for the child to learn his native language? Sufficient it cannot be since, by definition, it excludes some of the features that a child will need to learn in order to behave like a mature native speaker (reference to displaced objects and events and a 'normal' use of intonation, for example). Necessary it may be, but this still has to be proved. And even this seems to be unlikely, as not all parents make use of it to anything like the same extent, yet their children still eventually learn to talk.

However, without making a commitment to the necessity of experiencing motherese, it is still possible to ask whether the differences that can be observed in the manner and extent of parents' modification of their speech to young children are associated with differences in their children's learning. The collection of papers edited by Snow and Ferguson (1977), *Talking to Children*, contains two reports of studies with this orientation. The first by Newport *et al.* (1977) concentrated on syntactic properties of mothers' speech to three groups of children aged 12–15 months, 18–21 months and 24–27 months, relating differences between mothers' speech to amount of language growth over a six-month period. The results of their study do not offer much support for the hypothesis that motherese is a well-designed teaching language. On the contrary, they found little evidence that 'mothers tune their syntactic complexity to the growing language competence of their children through this crucial age of syntax acquisition' (p. 124). Furthermore, the influence on the children's learning of those features that were identified as specific to motherese was also very limited. In the second study, on the other hand, Cross (1977) found strong evidence of fine-tuning in mothers' speech to a specially selected sample of rapidly developing children. In this case, however, it was not syntax that was focused upon but semantic and discourse features of mothers' speech in relation to the level of comprehension displayed by the children, as measured by a set of items administered informally over the course of two recorded sessions. Cross concluded that 'the discourse adjustments found to be most sensitive to child level are precisely those that provide the child with ideal opportunities to learn the structure of his language' (p. 171).

We found these two studies provocative. Would Newport *et al.* have been more positive about the facilitating effect of mothers' speech if they had not focused so narrowly on syntax and if they had controlled for the effect of the child's stage of development on mothers' speech at the time of the data collection rather than *post hoc* by means of statistical treatment of their data? Was the fine-tuning that Cross found associated only with fast-developing children – and possibly a cause of that rapid development – or is it a feature of all parent–child inter-action and therefore not differentially facilitating? Ellis and Wells(1980) have tried to answer these questions from the Bristol data by means of a carefully controlled comparison of caretaker speech to three groups of children developing at different rates.

The three groups of 8–10 children were selected according to length of time that it took their Mean Length of Utterance (MLU) to increase by two morphemes, from 1.5 to 3.5.* Two fast developing groups made this gain in six months or less, but differed in the age at which they reached the lower limit: Early Fast Developers (EFD) were those who reached this point by 21 months or earlier; Last Fast Developers (LFD) were up to six months older by the time they reached the lower limit. The third group – the Slow Developers (SD) – took a minimum of twelve months to make the gain of two morphemes, independently of the age at which they reached the lower limit. Samples of caretaker speech were taken for all children at the time when they were at the lower limit and comparisons were made between the three groups in order to discover which features of caretaker speech, if any, were associated with rapid development.

As in the studies by Newport *et al.* and Cross already referred to, no significant differences were found between the three groups with respect to length or syntactic complexity, and although there was a trend for Early Fast Developers to receive more utterances referring to the immediate situation and, within these, a higher proportion that referred to activities being jointly undertaken by adult and child, the within group variation was too great for these differences to be statisti-cally significant. However, by contrast with Slow Developers, the EFD received a significantly higher proportion of utterances while engaged in routine household activities; they also received a significantly greater number of instructions and commands and of acknowledgements of their own utterances. Their caretakers were also more likely to repeat

---

* The actual values were chosen for convenience. However, they do correspond quite closely to the boundaries of the 'stage' within which mastery of the auxiliary verb is achieved.

or correct the children's utterances. Mean scores for the group of care-takers of LFD children were, in every case, intermediate between those of the EFD and SD groups.

A similar comparison between the three groups of caretakers when their children were at the upper MLU bound of 3.5 morphemes provided further confirmation of the existence of differences between the caretakers of fast and slow developing children. However, while at the second point of comparison the significant differences were still in the discourse functions and conversational style of caretaker speech rather than in length or syntactic complexity, it was no longer the proportion of commands and instructions that was the most significant discriminator between the groups, but rather statements and questions, and particularly tutorial questions, to which the questioner already knows the answer; EFD children received more utterances in all these functional categories.

These results are in keeping with those of both the studies referred to earlier in finding no significant difference between care-takers of fast and slow developers on the dimension of syntactic complexity. As Cross (1978) suggests, the register of adult speech to children may be fairly uniform on the syntactic dimension, with the particularly facilitating adaptations being largely in the selection of semantic content and discourse function. This suggestion is amply confirmed by the results of Ellis's study, where there are significant differences between the groups on both these dimensions. At the earlier stage of development the features of caretaker speech associated with early and fast development are its integration into a wide range of everyday activities which provide the context of joint action in which the child can match his understanding of familiar events with the linguistic encodings that are provided in the form of commands and instructions with respect to these same events. By the later stage of development, the association between rapid development and speech in a wide range of contexts remains unchanged, but now the emphasis has moved to the more strictly linguistic function of exchanging infor-mation and calling for the child to display his knowledge verbally – a function that will come to take on an even greater importance when he goes to school.

Following up the children during the first two years of schooling is the focus of one of our current investigations, as a continuing association between differences in caretaker speech and variation in school achievement is seen as an even more powerful test of our hypothesis of the importance of the child's early experience of linguistic interaction. Unfortunately, it is too early to report the results of this ongoing research, but an earlier follow-up study of twenty children from the older age group is suggestive of the sort of findings that we expect. In this earlier study we were concerned with the antecedents of success in learning to read, and data were collected from monthly observations in the class-room of the amount of time spent on different aspects of literacy and on the approaches to reading and the facilities provided in the different classes and schools that the children attended. Tests of knowledge about literacy (Clay 1972) and of reading attainment (Neale 1966; Carver 1970) were also administered at the beginning and end respectively of the two years at school. From the pre-school period we had various indices of the children's level of oral language development on entry to school, information about their interest in literacy and the interest shown by their parents and, of particular interest in the present context, an index of the quality of adult responsiveness to children's conversational initiations at the age of 3½ years.

This latter measure was devised by Evans (1977), who coded all utterances by parents in child-initiated sequences of conversation according to the extent to which they acknowledged and extended the meaning intended by the child's previous utterance. The hypothesis that she set out to test was that those children who received a greater proportion of utterances that helped them to develop and extend their meaning, would attain a more advanced stage of linguistic development by the time they entered school at 5 years of age. Four major categories of adult responding utterances were distinguished: inappropriate or non-occurring responses; procedural, where the adult requested some form of repetition or reformulation; plateau, where the child's meaning was acknowledged, but with no further addition; and developing, where the adult continued the theme proposed by the child in some relevant way. This latter category was further subdivided according to the extent to which the adult response encouraged the child to develop his initiation further. Each of these categories was assigned a weighting from 0 to 5 and the mean score calculated for each child's responses. Mean scores ranged from 0.46 to 2.62.

Considering the indices of language development at age 5 years for this small sample of twenty children, it is clear that Evans's hypothesis receives very substantial support. Quality of parental response, as measured by mean response score at 3½ years, is significantly associated with all the indices derived from spontaneous speech at age 5 ($p < .05$ in all cases). The association with tests of language comprehension at the same age is also positive but less significant (see Figure 7.2).

FIGURE 7.2 Inter-correlations between caretaker mean response score, oral language measures at 5 years and reading attainment at 7 years

	1	2	3	4	5	6	7	8	9	10	11	12	13
1 Mean Response Score at 3½ years	—												
2 Mean Length of Structured Utterance at 5	.51**	—											
3 Mean Length of Longest Utterance at 5	.55**	.86**	—										
4 Syntactic Complexity at 5	.61**	.75**	.70**	—									
5 Semantic Range at 5	.63**	.67**	.72**	.64**	—								
6 Semantic Modification at 5	.57**	.73**	.77**	.74**	.69**	—							
7 Functional Range at 5	.51**	.55**	.48**	.63**	.56**	.54**	—						
8 Comprehension Test at 5	.33	.21	.27	.18	.30	.26	.09	—					
9 English Picture Vocab. Test at 5	.48*	.16	.10	.37	.30	.37	.08	.37	—				
10 Child Interest in Literacy	.25	.05	-.10	.03	.06	.15	.29	.27	.38	—			
11 Parental Interest in Literacy	.60**	.45*	.39	.41	.46*	.47*	.56**	.23	.40	.38	—		
12 Knowledge of Literacy at 5	.51**	.33	.26	.05	.07	.35	.44*	.24	.40	.43	.77**	—	
13 Reading Attainment at 7	.63**	.33	.32	.32	.39	.53**	.43	.21	.45*	.40	.73**	.79**	—

N = 20

* p < .05　　** p < .01

This is not the place to discuss the results of the study of *Children Learning to Read* in detail (cf. Wells and Raban 1978) but it is interesting to note that while there is a positive but fairly weak association between reading attainment at age 7 and indices of oral language at age 5, the factors that are really strongly associated with reading attainment include two measures of parental interaction and involvement: the mean response score and parental interest in literacy (Figure 7.2). No school variables occur in this figure because, apart from the amount of time spent on non-literacy activities, they were not significantly associated with reading attainment. The best single predictor of success in reading after two years in school was the knowledge about literacy the child already possessed on entry to school and this was most strongly predicted by his parents' shared interest in literacy and by the quality of conversational interaction he experienced as measured at 3½ years.

The two studies together offer quite substantial evidence in support of an association between quantitative and qualitative differences in style of adult–child interaction and children's subsequent rate of language development – an association that apparently continues until well into the years of schooling. Some indication of the nature of these qualitative differences has been suggested in the studies reported here, involving children learning English in three different continents. In none of them is there any evidence of variation in syntactic modification in adult speech being associated with rate of development.* On the other hand, there is strong evidence of an association between the rate of the child's linguistic development and various semantic and discourse features of adult speech. Clearly, the crucial features do not remain constant over the course of development: features that may be facilitating at one stage may later cease to be important, only to be replaced by others that are more apt to the child's growing communicative ability. The studies reported here are suggestive of what these features may be, but a great deal more research will be required before the finer details become clear.

Although the evidence from the Bristol study and the other studies referred to can be taken as support for the widely held belief that school achievement is strongly influenced by differences in language ability on

* Since this paper was written, a small study has been reported by Furrow, Nelson and Benedict (1979) in which children's rate of syntactic development was found to be associated with differences between mothers in the syntactic complexity of their utterances: rapid development was associated, in particular, with a lower proportion of verbs, copulas and pronouns in mothers' speech. They also found rapid development to be associated with a high proportion of polar (yes/no) interrogatives, as did Newport *et al.* (1977) and a more recent study of the Bristol children (Wells 1980).

entry to school and that these in turn are largely determined by differences in parental use of language in the early years, I have two serious reservations about interpreting the evidence in a simple causal manner. The first concerns the assessment of language ability.

In an earlier attempt to explore the question 'What Makes for Successful Language Development?' (Wells 1978a), I reported a preliminary finding that different ways of assessing level of language development yielded surprisingly different rank orders among the same group of children. Subsequent analyses of our data have served only to confirm this finding. In the early stages of language development there is a strong relationship between syntactic, semantic and functional aspects of children's speech and between all of these and MLU. By the age of 5 years, however, this close interrelationship has weakened considerably, suggesting that the various dimensions of language, while clearly still interdependent, have become at the same time relatively independent. This is apparent from the intercorrelations between the various developmental indices in Figure 7.2. This is no doubt due in part to the fact that, by this age, most children have mastered the basic systems of language and the measures of development no longer discriminate between children so sensitively. However, it is still the case that particular children receive scores that lead to them being assigned quite widely differing ranks across the range of measures used.

From the point of view of assessing general level of linguistic ability this finding has considerable significance. First, it draws attention to the fact that command of a language is a complex of abilities and that individual children may be more advanced in one aspect of language and less in another. Secondly, it indicates the difficulty of finding one single measure that can give a really accurate assessment of individual children or which can accurately rank them with respect to each other. On the basis of our findings so far we have to conclude that there is no single measure that has continuing validity over the whole pre-school period. Language tests, in particular, we believe are likely to give a very biased estimate, with a serious danger of underestimating the abilities of lower-class children.

This conclusion must lead us to question the widespread use of tests and other forms of assessment of language development. The fact that some children develop earlier and faster than others is well-attested, but apart from those children whose retardation is the result of some physiological handicap, is there firm evidence that slower development has lasting effects of a cumulative kind, over and above the handicap of being labelled a slow learner? Do we not perhaps attach too much importance to relatively small differences between children in the rate at which they progress through the same stages of development?

Part of the explanation for the concern with inequalities in rate of learning is no doubt to be found in the competitive ethos that pervades formal education and our society in general. At all stages, merit is attributed to the children at the top of the class and the less successful are identified and assigned to the lower streams that form the conveyor belt to the poorly paid, low-status occupations. By providing instruments for assessment, and reporting the results of our research in terms of relative levels of achievement or progress, do we not contribute to this prevailing ethos – whether that is our intention or not?

Another, and more positive, use of assessment, is in the context of remediation, both clinical and educational. In the latter case, the aim is, while accepting the existing structure of society, to attempt to rectify some of the initial inequalities by identifying children who are considered to be developmentally retarded in order to provide remediation. However, the results of such attempts on a large scale have not been notably successful and it is doubtful whether they can be as long as the basic assumptions remain unchanged. Certainly, when this approach leads to whole groups of children being presumed to be retarded and their homes inadequate as a result of observed correlations between particular developmental measures, such as MLU or EPVT scores, and ascribed social group membership, we should pause to ask whether the diagnosis and treatment may not actually be contributing to the disease.

There is a third and more limited reason for focusing upon variation between children in assessments of development and that is to obtain a dependent variable for use in investigations of conditions necessary for – or at least facilitative of – development. The use of assessment here is a means to achieving insight into the nature and causes of development itself. This is the perspective intended in the discussion of variation in this paper. But even here, there must be some commitment to the important consequences of differential level of development at particular ages since the design of the research rests upon that assumption. There is, thus, an uneasy ambivalence inherent in almost all research that makes use of variation in rate of development.

My second reservation concerns the interpretation of the association between features of adult speech and children's differential rate of development. There is a considerable temptation to see this as evidence of a simple unidirectional causal relationship: the better adapted the adult's speech to the child's needs, the more effectively and quickly he will master the system. In theory, the argument seems very plausible. But it ignores two very important facts. The first is that for most if

not all children, a very high proportion of their experience of interaction is not particularly well adapted to their needs. Rather, it is
organized in terms of the needs of the parents: to keep the peace, to get
through the daily routines of feeding, dressing, cleaning etc., and much
of the speech that is addresssed to all children can be explained in
terms of such utilitarian objectives. Here again, the differences
between parents are not as great as the similarities, although this is not
to say that the residual variation is insignificant.

The second fact is that interaction, linguistic or otherwise, is
necessarily reciprocal: it follows, therefore, that if the behaviour of
parents influences the child's development, so too does the children's
behaviour influence that of their parents. This reciprocity of influence
is recognized in all the studies that have been referred to above, and is
the reason for controlling for the child's stage of development in comparisons of adults' speech styles. But this is still not the end of the
matter. We are all aware that some colleagues are easier to speak with
than others, although we should probably not attribute this so much to
differences between them in level of linguistic development, as to
differences of personality, intelligence or other such poorly understood
characteristics. If pressed we might also recognize that our own
personal characteristics were involved. The same is surely equally true
of both parents and children. While it is reasonable to assume that the
major responsibility for the 'quality' of the conversation between adult
and child rests with the adult, who has a greater range of options at his
or her disposal, it would be unwise to assume that there are not
differences between children, as there are between adults, in their
willingness and ability to sustain conversation, over and above
differences that are dependent on their level of linguistic ability.

In conclusion, we can be fairly certain that there is a positive
association between, on the one hand, the rate at which children master
their native language and in their ability to use their language skills to
engage in further learning and, on the other hand, the quality of
linguistic interaction they experience at home and at school. But what
causes the variation in quality of linguistic interaction is a more
complex question. Differences between parents – and later between
teachers – in their expectation about children's development and in the
role that they can play in facilitating that development are likely to be
an important factor, and although there is some evidence of an
association between such variation and social class, there is also ample
evidence of families that do not conform to such class stereotypes, so we
should certainly not succcumb to the temptation to treat class membership as an explanation in itself. Equally important, it seems to me, are

differences between adults and children alike in the interest and enjoyment they find in interaction with each other; this is partly dependent
upon the adults' skill in matching his or her contribution to the child's
level of ability, but there seem to be other factors involved, such as
freedom from other demands on the adult's attention, state of health,
both physical and mental, and match or mismatch in what I can only
refer to generally as personality. I do not wish to suggest that such
qualitative differences must be accepted as immutable, but before we
attempt to intervene on a large scale, we need to find out a great deal
more about what influences the ways in which adults and children talk
to each other, and why some examples of interaction seem to be so
much more successful than others.

References

ARMSTRONG, G. (1975), 'An Experiment in Early Learning', *Concern (National Children's Bureau)* **18,** pp. 20–5.

AUERBACH, A. B. (1968), *Parents Learn Through Discussion: Principles and Practices of Parent Group Education,* Wiley, New York.

BALL, S., and BOGATZ, G. (1970), *The First Year of Sesame Street: An Evaluation,* Educational Testing Service, Princeton, New Jersey.

BANNISTER, D., and BOTT, M. (1973), 'Evaluating the Person', in P. Kline (ed.), *New Approaches in Psychological Measurement,* Wiley, London.

BARNES, J. (ed.) (1975), *Educational Priority. Vol. 3: Curriculum Innovations in London's EPAs,* HMSO.

BARR, J. (1974), 'Napoli, Bedfordshire', *New Society,* 12 April.

BATES, E. (1976), 'Pragmatics and Sociolinguistics in Child Language', in D. M. Morehead and A. E. Morehead (eds), *Normal and Deficient Child Language,* University Park Press, Baltimore.

BEREITER, C., and ENGELMANN, S. (1966), *Teaching Disadvantaged Children in the Pre-School,* Prentice-Hall, New Jersey.

BERNSTEIN, B. (1971), *Class, Codes and Controls,* Routledge & Kegan Paul, London.

BLANK, M. (1974), 'Cognitive Functions of Language in the Pre-school Years', *Developmental Psychology* **10,** pp. 229–45.

BLANK, M. and SOLOMON, F. (1968), 'A Tutorial Language Program to Develop Abstract Thinking in Socially Disadvantaged Pre-school Children', *Child Development* **39,** pp. 379–89.

BLOOM, L. A. (1970), *Language Development: Form and Function in Emerging Grammars,* MIT Press, Cambridge, Mass.

BLOOM, L. A. (1973), *One Word at a Time,* Mouton, The Hague.

BLUMA, S. M. *et al.* (1976), *Portage Guide to Early Education: Manual,* Co-operative Educational Service Agency 12, Portage, Wisconsin.

BOGATZ, G. A., and BALL, S. (1971), *The Second Year of Sesame Street: a Continuing Evaluation, Vols. 1 and 2,* Educational Testing Service, Princeton, New Jersey.

BOISSEVAIN, J. (1971), *The Italians in Montreal. Social Adjustment in a Plural Society*, Studies of the Royal Commission on Bilingualism and Biculturalism **7**, Printing and Publishing Supplies and Services, Ottawa.

BRAINE, M. D. S. (1974), 'Length Constraints, Reduction Rules and Holophrastic Processes in Children's Word Combinations, *Journal of Verbal Learning and Verbal Behaviour* **13**, pp. 448–57.

BRANDIS, W., and BERNSTEIN, B. (1974), *Selection and Control*, Routledge & Kegan Paul, London.

BRIDGES, A. (1979), 'Directing Two Year Olds' Attention; Some Clues to Understanding', *Journal of Child Language* **6**, pp. 211–26.

BRIM, O. G. (1965), *Education for Child Rearing*, Free Press, New York.

BRONFENBRENNER, U. (1974a), *A Report on Longitudinal Evaluations of Pre-School Programmes, Vol. 2 – Is Early Intervention Effective?* Department of Health, Education and Welfare, Washington DC.

BRONFENBRENNER, U. (1974b), *Two Worlds of Childhood*, Penguin, Harmondsworth.

BRONFENBRENNER, U. (1975), 'Reality and Research in the Ecology of Human Development', *Proc. Amer. Philos. Socy* **119**, pp. 439–69.

BRONFENBRENNER, U. (1978), *Proposal for an International Intervention Project*, National Institute of Education, Washington.

BROWN, J. (1970), *The Unmelting Pot*, Macmillan, London.

BROWN, R. (1968), 'The Development of 'wh' Questions in Child Speech', *Journal of Verbal Learning and Verbal Behaviour* **7**, pp. 279–90.

BROWN, R. (1973), *A First Language: The Early Stages*, Allen & Unwin, London.

BROWN, R., and BELLUGI, U. (1964), 'Three Processes in the Child's Acquisition of Syntax', in E. Lenneberg (ed.), *New Directions in the Study of Language*, MIT Press, Cambridge, Mass.

BROWN, R., and FRASER, C. (1964), 'The Acquisition of Syntax', in U. Bellugi and R. Brown (eds), *The Acquisition of Language*, Monograph of the Society for Research in Child Development, vol. 29, no. 1.

BRUNER, J. S. *et al.* (1966), *Studies in Cognitive Growth*, John Wiley, New York.

BRUNER, J. S. (1976), 'Nature and Uses of Immaturity', in J. S. Bruner *et al.* (eds), *Play*, Penguin, Harmondsworth.

BRUNER, J. S. (1980), *Under Five in Britain*, Grant McIntyre.

BRYANT, P. E. (1973), 'What the Young Child Has to Learn about Logic', in R. A. Hinde and J. Stevenson-Hinde (eds), *Constraints on Learning*, Academic Press, London.

BULLOCK, SIR A. (Chairman) (1975), *A Language for Life: Report of the Committee of Enquiry*, Department of Education and Science, HMSO.

CARVER, C. (1970), *Word Recognition Test*, University of London Press.

CAZDEN, C. (1968), 'The Aquisition of Noun and Verb Inflections', *Child Development* **39**, pp. 433–8.

CAZDEN, C. (1974), 'Concentrated vs. Contrived Encounters: Suggestions for Language Assessment in Early Childhood Education', in A. Davies (ed.), *Language and Learning in Early Childhood*, Heinemann Educational Books (1977).

CHAZAN, M. (1978), 'Education and preparation for parenthood', in V. Carver (ed.), *Child Abuse: A Study Text*, Open University Press, Milton Keynes.

CHAZAN, M. (1979), 'Young Children with Special Needs: Home-Based Projects', in A. F. Laing (ed.), *Young Children with Special Needs*, Department of Education, University College of Swansea.

CHAZAN, M., LAING, A. F., COX, T., JACKSON, S., and LLOYD, G. (1976), *Studies of Infant School Children: Deprivation and School Progress*, Basil Blackwell, Oxford (for the Schools Council).

CHAZAN, M., LAING, A. F., and JACKSON, S. (1971), *Just Before School*, Basil Blackwell, Oxford (for Schools Council).

CHILD, I. (1943), *Italian or American?* Russel & Russel, New York.

CICOUREL, A. V. (1974), 'Some Basic Theoretical Issues in the Assessment of the Child's Performance in Testing and Classroom Settings', in A. Cicourel *et al.*, *Language Use and School Performance*, Academic Press, London.

CLARK, R. (1974), 'Performing Without Competence', *Journal of Child Language* **1**, pp. 1–10.

CLARK, R. (1975a), 'Adult Theories, Child Strategies and Their Implications for the Language Teacher', in J. P. B. Allen and S. Pit Corder (eds), *Edinburgh Course in Applied Linguistics*, vol. 2, Oxford University Press, London.

CLARK, R. (1975b), Review of Lois Bloom 'One word at a time', *Journal of Child Language* **2**, pp. 169–93.

CLARK, R. (1976), 'A Report on Methods of Longitudinal Data Collection', *Journal of Child Language* **3**, pp. 457–9.

CLARK, R. (1977), 'What's the Use of Imitation?' *Journal of Child Language* **4**, pp. 341–58.

CLARK, R. (1978), 'Some Even Simpler Ways to Learn to Talk', in N. Waterson and C. Snow (eds), *The Development of Communication*, Wiley, London.

CLARK, R., HUTCHESON, S., and VAN BUREN, P. (1974), 'Comprehension and Production in Language Acquisition', *Journal of Linguistics* **10**, pp 39–54.

CLARKE, A. M., and CLARKE, A. D. B. (1976), *Early Experience: Myth and Evidence*, Open Books, London.

CLAY, M. M. (1972), *The Early Detection of Reading Difficulties: A Diagnostic Survey*, Heinemann Educational Books, London.

COLEMAN, J. S. *et al.* (1966), *Equality of Educational Opportunity*, Government Printing Office, Washington DC.

COOK-GUMPERZ, J., and GUMPERZ, J. J. (1978), 'Context in Children's Speech', in N. Waterson and C. Snow (eds), *The Development of Communication*, Wiley, London.

CROSS, T. G. (1977), 'Mothers' Speech Adjustments: The Contribution of Selected Child Listener Variables', in C. Snow and C. Ferguson (eds), *Talking to Children: Language Input and Acquisition*, Cambridge University Press.

CROSS, T. G. (1978), 'Mothers' Speech and its Association with Rate of Linguistic Development in Young Children', in N. Waterson and C. Snow (eds), *The Development of Communication*, Wiley, London.

CUNNINGHAM, C. C. (1975), 'Parents as Therapists and Educators', in C. C. Kiernan and M. P. Woodford (eds), *Behaviour Modification with the Severely Retarded*, Association of Scientific Publishers, Amsterdam.

DAVÉ, R. H. (1963), 'The Identification and Measurement of Environmental Process Variables that are Related to Educational Achievement', Ph.D. dissertation, University of Chicago.

DAVIE, R., BUTLER, N., and GOLDSTEIN, H. (1972), *From Birth to Seven*, Longman, London.

DE MAURO, T. (1963), *Storia linguistica dell'Italia unita*, Laterza, Bari.

DEPARTMENT OF EDUCATION AND SCIENCE (1975), *A Language for Life* (The Bullock Report), HMSO, London.

DONACHY, W. (1972), 'Promoting Cognitive Growth in Culturally Deprived Pre-School Children', M.Ed. thesis, University of Glasgow.

DONACHY, W. (1976), 'Parent Participation in Pre-school Education', *Brit. J. Educ. Psychol*, **46,** pp. 1–39.

DONALDSON, M. (1978), *Children's Minds*, Fontana, London.

DORE, J., FRANKLIN, M. B., MILLER, R. T., and RAMER, A. L. H. (1976), 'Transitional Phenomena in Early Language Acquisition', *Journal of Child Language* **3,** pp. 13–28.

DOUGLAS, J. W. B. (1964), *The Home and the School*, MacGibbon & Kee, London.

ELLIOT, C. D., MURRAY, D. J., and PEARSON, L. S. (1978), The British Ability Scales. *Manual 3 Directions for Administration and Scoring*, National Foundation for Educational Research, Windsor.

ELLIS, R. J., and WELLS, C. G. (1980), 'Enabling Factors in Adult–Child Discourse', *First Language*, 1, pp. 46–62.

ENTWISTLE, N. J. (1979), 'Stages, Levels, Styles or Strategies: Dilemmas in the Description of Thinking', *Educational Review* **31,** pp. 123–32.

EVANS, J. V. (1977), 'The Significance of Adult Feedback on Child Language Development', unpublished M.Ed. dissertation, University of Bristol School of Education.

FENN, G. (1978), Review of D. M. Morehead and A. E. Morehead (eds), 'Normal and Deficient Child Language', *Journal of Child Language* **5,** pp. 539–43.

FERRIER, L. J. (1978), 'Some Observations of Error in Context', in Waterson and Snow (eds), *The Development of Communication*, op. cit.

FISHMAN, J. A. (1967), 'Bilingualism with and without Diglossia, Diglossia with and without Bilingualism', *Journal of Social Issues* **23,** 2.

FRASER, E. (1959), *Home Environment and the School*, University of London Press.

FURROW, D., NELSON, K., and BENEDICT, H. (1979), 'Mothers' Speech to Children and Syntactic Development: Some Simple Relationships', *Journal of Child Language* **6,** pp. 423–42.

GAHAGAN, D. M., and GAHAGAN. G. A. (1970), *Talk Reform*, Routledge & Kegan Paul, London.

GARDNER, R. A., and GARDNER, B. T. (1975), 'Early Signs of Language in Child and Chimpanzee', *Science* **187,** pp. 752–3.

GARNICA, O. K. (1977), 'Some Prosodic and Paralingual Features of Speech to Young Children', in C. Snow and D. Ferguson (eds), *Talking to Children: Language Input and Acquisition*, Cambridge University Press.

GATHERCOLE, C. E. (1968), *Assessment in Clinical Psychology*, Penguin, Harmondsworth.

GOFFMAN, E. (1957), 'Alienation from Interaction', *Human Relations* **10,** pp. 47–60.

GOLDIN-MEADOWS, S. (1979), 'Structure in a Manual Communication System Developed without a Conventional Language Model: Language without a Helping Hand', in H. Whittaker and H. A. Whittaker (eds), *Studies in Neurolinguistics*, vol. IV, Academic Press, New York.

GORDON, I. J. (1968), *Parental Involvement in Compensatory Education*, University of Illinois Press.

GORDON, I. J. (1973), *An Early Intervention Project: a Longitudinal Look*, Institute for Development of Human Resources, University of Florida.

GORDON, I. J. (1975), *The Infant Experience*, C. E. Merrill, Columbus, Ohio.

GRIFFITHS, P. (1979), 'A Study of the Acquisition of Affirmation', Child Language Seminar, 2–3 April, Reading.

HALLIDAY, M. A. K. (1975), *Learning how to Mean. Explorations in the Development of Language*, Edward Arnold, London.

HALSEY, A. H. (ed.) (1972), *Educational Priority. Vol 1: EPA – Problems and Policies*, HMSO.

HEBER, R., and GARBER, H. (1975), 'Progress Report II: an Experiment in the Prevention of Cultural–Familial Retardation', in D. A. Primrose (ed.), *Proceedings of the 3rd Congress of the International Association for the Scientific Study of Mental Deficiency*, Polish Medical Publishers, Warsaw.

HESS, R., and SHIPMAN, V. C. (1965), 'Early Experience and the Socialization of Cognitive Modes in Children', *Child Development* **36**, pp. 869–76.

HORGAN, D. (1978), 'How to Answer Questions when You've got Nothing to Say', *Journal of Child Language* **5,** pp. 159–65.

HUTTENLOCHER, J. (1974), 'The Origins of Language Comprehension', in R. S. Solso (ed.), *Theories in Cognitive Psychology*, Loyola Symposium, Wiley.

ITA REPORT (1971), *Reactions to Sesame Street in Britain, 1971, Part I*, Independent Television Authority in association with the National Council for Educational Technology, London.

JEFFREE, D. M., and MCCONKEY, R. (1976a), *Let Me Speak*, Souvenir Press, London.

JEFFREE, D. M., and MCCONKEY, R. (1976b), *P.I.P. Development Charts*, Hodder & Stoughton, London.

JENCKS, D. (1972), *Inequality*, Allen Lane, London.

KEENAN, E. O. (1974), 'Conversational Competence in Children', *Journal of Child Language* **1,** pp. 163–83.

KELLAGHAN, T. (1977), *The Evaluation of an Intervention Programme for Disadvantaged Children*, NFER.

KELLAGHAN, T., and ARCHER, P. (1973), *A Home Intervention Project for Two and Three Year Old Disadvantaged Children*, E. Res. Centre, St Patrick's College, Dublin 9.

KELLAGHAN, T., and ARCHER, P. (1975), *A Study of Home Intervention for the Pre-School Disadvantaged*, E. Res. Centre, St Patrick's College, Dublin 9.

KELLY, G. H. (1955), *The Psychology of Personal Constructs. Vol. 1: A Theory of Personality*, Norton, New York.

KING, R. (1977), 'The Italian Connection', *Geography Magazine*, vol. XLIV, April 1977.

KOHN, M. L. (1969), *Class and Conformity: A Study in Values*, Donsey Press, Illinois.

LABOV, W. (1972), *Sociolinguistic Patterns*, Pennsylvania University Press, Philadelphia.

LAZAR, I. (1977), 'Preliminary Findings of the Developmental Continuity Longitudinal Study', paper presented at Office of Child Development 'Parents, Children and Continuity' Conference, Texas, May 1977.

LEPSCHY, A. L., and G. (1977), *The Italian Language Today*, Hutchinson, London.

LEVENSTEIN, P. (1970), 'Cognitive Growth in Pre-schoolers through Verbal Interaction with Mothers', Amer. J. Orthopsychiat. **40,** pp. 426–32.

LEVENSTEIN, P. (1972), 'But Does it Work in Homes Away from Home?' *Theory into Practice*, vol. XI, no. 3, Verbal Interaction Project.

LEVENSTEIN, P. (1975), *The Mother–Child Home Program*, Verbal Interaction Project, New York.

LEVENSTEIN, P. (1978), *Developmental Continuity Consortium*, Follow-up Study. Verbal Interaction Projection, New York.

LEWIN, R. (1977), '"Head-start" pays off', *New Scientist*, 3 March.

LEWIS, E. G. (1970), 'Immigrants, Their Language and Development', *Trends in Education* **19.**

LIMBER, J. (1973), 'The Genesis of Complex Sentences', in T. E. Moore (ed.), *Cognitive Development and the Acquisition of Language*, Academic Press, New York.

LOVE, J. *et al.* (1976), *National Home Start Evaluation: Final Report: Findings and Implications*, ABT Associates Ltd, Cambridge, Mass.

MCCAIL, G. (1981), *Mother Start*, The Scottish Council for Research in Education, Edinburgh.

McGARRIGLE, J., and DONALDSON, M. (1975), 'Conservation Accidents', *Cognition* **3,** pp. 341–50.

MACNAMARA, J. (1972), 'Cognitive Basis of Language Learning in Infants', *Psychological Review* **79,** pp. 1–13.

McNEILL, D. (1966), 'Developmental Psycholinguistics', in F. Smith and G. Miller (eds), *The Genesis of Language: a Psycholinguistic Approach*, MIT Press, Cambridge, Mass.

McNEILL, D., and McNEILL, N. B. (1968), 'What Does a Child Mean when He Says "No"?', in G. M. Zale (ed.), *Proceedings of the Conference on Language and Language Behaviour*, Appleton Century Crofts, New York.

MASLOW, A. H. (1954), *Motivation and Personality*, Harper, New York.

MENYUK, P. (1964), 'Comparison of Grammar of Children with Functionally Deviant and Normal Speech', *Journal of Speech and Hearing Research* **7,** pp. 109–21.

MIONI, A. (1975), 'Per una sociolinguistica italiana: note di un non sociologo', preface to J. A. Fishman, *La sociologia del linguaggio* Officina Editrice, Roma.

MIONI, A. (1979), 'La situazione sociolinguistica italiana: lingua dialetti, italiani regionali', in A. Colombo (ed.), *Guida all'educazione linguistica*, Zanichelli, Bologna.

MORRISON, C. M., WATT, J. S., and LEE, T. R. (eds) (1974), *Educational Priority. Vol. 5: EPA – A Scottish Study*, HMSO.

NATIONAL CHILDREN'S BUREAU (1977a), *Highlight No. 29, Educational Home Visiting.*

NATIONAL CHILDREN'S BUREAU (1977b), *Educational Home Visiting: Some Local Authority and Voluntary Schemes* (mimeo), NCB, 8 Wakley Street, London.

NEALE, M. O. (1966), *Neale Analysis of Reading Ability*, 2nd ed., Macmillan Education, London.

NELSON, K. (1973), *Structure and Strategy in Learning to Talk*, Monograph for the Society for Research in Child Development, no. 149, vol. 38, nos. 1 and 2.

NEWPORT, E. L., GLEITMAN, H., and GLEITMAN, L. R. (1977), 'Mother I'd rather Do It Myself: Some Effects and Non-effects of Maternal Speech Style', in C. Snow and C. Ferguson (eds), *Talking to Children: Language Input and Acquisition*, Cambridge University Press.

NEWSON, J., and E. (1968), *Four Years Old in an Urban Community*, Penguin, Harmondsworth.

NEWSON, J., and E. (1978), *Perspectives on School at Seven Years Old*, Allen & Unwin, London.

O'DELL, S. (1974), 'Training Parents in Behaviour Modification: A Review', *Psychol. Bull.* **81,** pp. 418–33.

ORNE, M. T. (1973), 'Communication by the Total Experimental Situation: Why It Is Important, How It Is Evaluated, and Its Significance for the Ecological Validity of Findings', in P. Pliner, L. Krames and T. Alloway (eds), *Communication and Affect, Language and Thought*, Academic Press, New York.

PAGE, E. B. (1972), 'Miracle in Milwaukee: Raising the I.Q.', *Educational Researcher* **1,** pp. 8–16.

PALMER, F. H. (1977), 'The Effects of Early Childhood in Educational Intervention on School Performance', paper prepared for The President's Commission on Mental Health.

PARLETT, M., and HAMILTON, D. (1972), *Evaluation as Illumination: A New Approach to the Study of Innovatory Programmes*, Centre for Research in the Educational Sciences, University of Edinburgh, Occasional Paper.

PEAKER, G. F. (1967), The Regression Analyses of The National Survey, Appendix 4 in 'Plowden Report' *Children and Their Primary Schools. Vol 2: Research and Surveys*, pp. 179–221. HMSO.

PEAKER, G. F. (1971), *The Plowden Children Four Years Later*, NFER, Windsor.

PEAKER, G. F. (1975), *An Empirical Study of Education in Twenty One Countries: A Technical Report*, Wiley, New York.

PEEL, E. (1978), 'Generalising through the Verbal Medium', *British Journal of Educational Psychology* **48**, pp. 36–46.

PELLEGRINI, G. B. (1960), 'Tra lingua e dialetto in Italia', *Studi mediolatini e volgari* **8.**

PELLEGRINI, G. B. (1962), 'L'italiano regionale', *Cultura e scuola* **5.**

PELLEGRINI, G. B. (1974), 'Dal dialetto alla lingua' (esperienze di un veneto settentrionale), *Dal Dialetto alla lingua. Atti del IX convegno per gli studi dialettali italiani*, Pisa.

PLOWDEN REPORT (1966), *Central Advisory Council on Education, Children and their Primary Schools*. Vols I and II, HMSO.

QUIGLEY, H. (1971), 'Reactions of Eleven Nursery Teachers and Assistants to the Peabody Language Development Kit', *British Journal of Educational Psychology* **41**, pp. 155–62.

RATNER, N., and BRUNER, J. (1978), 'Games, Social Exchange and the Acquisition of Language', *Journal of Child Language* **5**, pp. 391–401.

RAVEN, J. (1976), *Pupil Motivation and Values*, Irish Association for Curriculum Development, Dublin.

RAVEN, J. (1977), *Education, Values and Society*, H. K. Lewis, London; the Psychological Corporation, New York.

RAVEN, J. (1980), *Parents, Teachers and Children*, Hodder and Stoughton, Sevenoaks.

ROSEN, C., and ROSEN, H. (1973), *The Language of Primary School Children*, Penguin, Harmondsworth.

ROSEN, H., and BURGESS, T. (1981), *Languages and Dialects of London School-children*, Ward Lock, London.

ROSENTHAL, R., and JACOBSON, L. (1968), *Pygmalion in the Classroom: Teacher Expectation and Pupils' Intellectual Development*, Holt, Rinehart & Winston, New York.

RUNNYMEDE TRUST (1972), *The Invisible Immigrants*, Runnymede Trust Paper.

RUNNYMEDE TRUST (1976), *Linguistic Minorities In Britain*, Briefing Paper 2/76 (by K. Campbell-Platt, rev. by S. Nicholas 1978).

RUTTER, M., MAUGHAN, B., MORTIMORE, P., and OUSTON, J. (1979), *Fifteen Thousand Hours*, Open Books, London.

RYAN, J. (1972), 'I.Q. The Illusion of Objectivity', in K. Richardson and D. Spears (eds), *Race, Culture and Intelligence*, Penguin, Harmondsworth.

RYAN, J. (1973), 'Interpretation and Imitation in Early Language

Development', in R. A. Hinde and J. Stevenson-Hinde (eds), *Constraints on Learning*, Academic Press, London.

SCHAEFER, E. S. (1972), 'Parents as Educators: Evidence from Cross-sectional, Longitudinal and Intervention Research', *Young Children* **27,** 227–39.

SHUGAR, G. W. (1978), 'Text Analysis as an Approach to the Study of Early Linguistic Operations', in N. Waterson and C. Snow (eds), *The Development of Communication*, Wiley, London.

SKUTNABB-KANGAS, T. (1976), *Teaching Migrant Children Their Mother Tongue and Learning the Language of the Host Country in the Context of the Socio-cultural Situation of the Migrant Family*, Tutkimuksia Research Reports, Tampere, Finland.

SMITH, G. (ed.) (1975), *Educational Priority, Vol. 4: EPA – The West Riding Project*, HMSO.

SMITH, J., KUSHLICK, A., and GLOSSOP, C. (1977), *The Wessex Portage Project: a Home Teaching Service for Families with a Pre-school Mentally Handicapped Child Parts I and II*, Wessex Regional Health Authority, Health Care Evaluation Research Team.

SNOW, C. (1977), 'Mothers' Speech Research: from Input to Acquisition', in C. Snow and C. Ferguson (eds), *Talking to Children: Language Input and Acquisition*, Cambridge University Press.

SNOW, C., and FERGUSON, C. (eds) (1977), *Talking to Children: Language Input and Acquisition*, Cambridge University Press.

SPEARMAN, C. (1927), *The Abilities of Man*, Macmillan.

SPONZA, L. (ed.) (1979), Special Issue on Italian Immigration, Association of Teachers of Italian, Autumn.

STARK, R. (1978), 'Features of Infant Sounds: the Emergence of Cooing', *Journal of Child Language* **5,** pp. 379–90.

STEFFENSEN, M. S. (1978), 'Satisfying Inquisitive Adults: Some Simple Methods of Answering Yes/No Questions', *Journal of Child Language* **5,** pp. 221–36.

STOKOE, W. C. (1977), 'Verbal and Nonverbal Sign Language', paper given at Edinburgh University in the Psychology Department, 18 November 1977.

SWAIN, M., and CUMMINS, J. (1979), 'Bilingualism, Cognitive Functioning and Education', *Language Teaching and Linguistics: Abstracts* **12** 1.

THE TIMES (1960), 'Little Italy in Bedford', 29 September.

TIZARD, B. (1974a), *Early Childhood Education: a Review and Discussion of Research in Britain*, NFER, Windsor.

TIZARD, B. (1974b), 'Staff and Parent Talk to Young Children', in B. Tizard (ed.), *Early Childhood Education*, NFER.

TOSI, A. (1978), 'L'insegnamento della lingua medre ai figli dei lavoratori immigrati in Gran Bretagna con particolare referimento al gruppo italiano', *Rassegna Italiana di Linguistica Applicata* **10**.

TOSI, A. (1979a), 'Li matune di Bedforde o le fondamenta della comunita italiana di Bedford', in Sponza (ed.) (1979).

TOSI, A. (1979b), 'Mother Tongue Teaching for the Children of Migrants', *Language Teaching and Linguistics: Abstracts* **12** 4.

TOSI, A. (forthcoming 1), 'Bilinguismo, transfert e interferenze. Considerazioni sul processo di acquisizione dell'italiano in figli di emigrati bilingui in inglese e dialetto campano', paper from a conference on 'Linguistica Contrastiva', May 1979, convened by Societa di Linguistica Italiana, Asti (forthcoming in Atti del Congresso).

TOSI, A. (forthcoming 2), 'Aspetti cross-culturali dell'interferenza morfosemantica nel bilinguismo etnico', paper prepared for the conference 'Linguistica e Antropologia' convened by Societa di Linguistica Italiana, Lecce, May 1980 (forthcoming in Atti del Congresso).

TOSI, A. (forthcoming 3), 'The Relationship between Learning Processes and Teaching Methods in Developing Migrants' Children Bilingual Literacy', paper presented at the Congress Sprachen und Fremdsprachenunterricht in Europa convened by Fachverband Moderne Fremdsprachen, April 1980, Hamburg.

TOUGH, J. (1973), *Focus on Meaning: Talking with Some Purpose to Young Children*, Allen & Unwin.

TOUGH, J. (1976), *Listening to Children Talking*, Ward Lock, London.

TOUGH, J. (1977), *Talking and Learning*, Ward Lock, London.

TOUKOMAA, P., and SKUTNABB-KANGAS. T. (1977), *The Intensive Teaching of the Mother Tongue to Migrant Children of Pre-school Age and Children in the Lower Level of Comprehensive School*, The Finnish National Commission for UNESCO, Helsinki.

TRUDGILL, P. (1974), *Sociolinguistics, An Introduction*, Penguin, Harmondsworth.

TRUMPER, J. (1977), 'Ricostruzione nell'Italia Settentrionale: sistemi consonantici. Considerazioni sociolinguistica nella dicronia', in R. Simone and U. Vignuzzi (eds), Atti del Convegno Internazionale di Studi, Societa di Linguistica Italiana, *Problemi della ricostruzione in linguistica*, Roma.

TRUMPER, J. (in press), 'La zona. Lausberg ed il problema della frammentazione linguistica', Convegno S.L.I. Cagliari, 1977.

TUDDENHAM, D. (1971), 'Theoretical Regularities and Individual Idiosyncracies', in D. R. Green, M. P. Ford and G. B. Flamer (eds), *Measurement and Piaget*, McGraw-Hill, New York.

UZGIRIS, I. C., and MCV. HUNT, J. (1975), *Assessment in Infancy. Ordinal Scales of Psychological Development,* University of Illinois Press, Chicago.

VAN DER EYKEN, W. (1982), *The Young Child in the Community,* Penguin, Harmondsworth.

VOLTERRA, V., and TAESCHNER, T. (1978), 'The Acquisition and Development of Language by Bilingual Children', *Journal of Child Language* **5,** pp. 311–26.

VYGOTSKY, L. (1962), *Thought and Language,* MIT Press, Cambridge, Mass.

WALKER, E. C. (1963), 'Bilingualism in Bedford', *The Teacher,* 19 July.

WARDEN, D. (1979), 'Children's Understanding of *Ask* and *Tell*: A Reappraisal', unpublished manuscript.

WEDGE, P., and PROSSER, H. (1973), *Born to Fail?* Arrow Books, London.

WELLS, C. G. (1977), 'Language Use and Educational Success', *Nottingham Linguistic Circular* **6** 2, pp. 29–50.

WELLS, C. G. (1978a), 'What Makes for Successful Language Development?' in R. Campbell and P. Smith (eds), *Advances in the Psychology of Language,* Plenum Publishing Co., New York.

WELLS, C. G. (1978b), *Language Development in Pre-School Children,* Final Report to the SSRC.

WELLS, C. G. (1979), 'Learning and Using the Auxiliary Verb in English', in V. Lee (ed.), *Language Development,* Croom Helm, London.

WELLS, C. G. (1980), 'Adjustments in Adult–Child Conversation: Some Effects of Interaction', in H. Giles, W. P. Robinson and P. M. Smith (eds), *Language: Social-Psychological Perspectives,* Pergamon Press, Oxford.

WELLS, C. G., and RABAN, B. (1978), *Children Learning to Read,* Final Report to the SSRC.

WELLS, C. G., and WOLL, B. (1979), 'The Development of Meaning Relations in Children's Speech', paper given at the Child Language Seminar, Reading, April 1979.

WHITE, B. *et al.* (1976), 'Competence and Experience', in I. C. Uzgiris (ed.), *The Structuring of Experience,* Plenum Publishing Co., New York.

WOLL, B. (1979), 'Sex as a Variable in Child Language Research', *Bristol Working Papers in Language 1.*

WOODHEAD, M. (1976a), *Intervening in Disadvantage: a challenge for nursery education,* NFER, Windsor.

WOODHEAD, M. (1976b), *An Experiment in Nursery Education,* NFER, Windsor.

Index